I dedicate this book to my Crossover Church leadership team. Every time I get inspired with crazy big ideas to Love Our City - you jump in to collaborate, dream and make the vision even better. This has touched more lives in our city than we would have ever imagined and the Love Our City movement is now growing around the world. Thank you for your prayer, support and hard work. The best is yet to come!

TABLE OF CONTENTS

30 Days

LEARNING TO LOVE OUR NEIGHBOR AS WE LOVE OURSELVES.

TOMMY "URBAN D." KYLLONEN

Tranzlation Leadership
Tampa, Florida

Tranzlation Leadership
1235 E. Fowler Ave. Tampa, Florida 33612
© 2018 by Tommy Kyllonen

While any stories in this book are true, some names and identifying information
may have been changed to protect the privacy of individuals.

Cover + Interior Design: Edward "Spec" Bayonet | iAMbayo.net

Logo Design: Josue Marrero / GMI Studios

Photography: Crossover Church Social Media Team

ISBN: 978-1-7327782-0-7 (print)

ISBN: 978-1-7327782-1-4 (ebook)

ISBN: 978-1-7327782-2-1 (audio download)

Printed in the United States of America

www.loveourcitybook.com

thought I was just going to play basketball. But, what happened on that court in the summer of 1993 changed someone's eternity and helped shape the direction of my ministry. As I was shooting around I connected with this guy named Carlos. We talked about basketball and Hip-Hop. I was home on summer break from college where I was studying to be in youth ministry. I weaved God into the conversation as I told him about the career path I was in school for. Carlos shared with me that he had never attended a Christian church in his life. His family was Catholic, but only by title. He had only attended a Catholic church a few times when he was a kid. I invited him to come to the church I was attending. He accepted. I was excited. I had a seat saved for him and I told a few people that my new friend Carlos was coming to church. I kept looking back and kept looking back, but Carlos never showed. The next week I ran into him again at the basketball courts and asked him what happened on Sunday and he told me that he forgot and that he would come this Sunday. You can guess what happened that Sunday. No show.

The following week when I saw him I got his phone number and I told him I would come and pick him up for church. He only lived 3 blocks away from the church, but I offered him a ride to make sure he would really come this time. That Sunday Carlos came to church and it was a day I'll never forget. I realized how weird some Christians are. I grew up in church, so I was used to some of the traditions, even if they weren't my style. But, Carlos had never stepped foot in that type of environment. So that day I put myself in his shoes and tried to experience it through his eyes. It was painful. First off, I realized our hospitality was lacking, as he wasn't welcomed by anyone. Secondly, I noticed that he was dressed in jeans and a T-Shirt and everyone else was dressed up. I thought it wouldn't be a big deal, but it seemed to be as others were staring. This immediately made him feel awkward. On top of that he was the only Hispanic in the room. I knew the diversity of the church was almost non-existent, but I was hopeful he would be embraced. Not really the result. Then came all of the questions. What does that song mean? Why did they say that? He wasn't complaining. He just had honest questions. Some of them I could easily answer, and some of them had me thinking, "Why do we do that?"

It was an epiphany moment that rocked me to the core. It began to shape my ministry philosophy for the future. I didn't have all the details mapped out, but I knew I wanted to create a church that would truly Love Our City and when they came to our house they would be welcomed. They would be able to come in and be able to connect with the music, the language and the dress code. They would be able to walk in and see someone that looked like them. This became super important to me. Our church said they wanted to show the love of Christ to the community, but there wasn't anything tangible that we ever did. Carlos lived just three blocks away and nobody in the church looked like him, his family or many of his neighbors. This forever changed my thinking about my church and my neighbors.

I'm grateful you picked up this book and you are going on this 30-day journey with us to learn to better love our neighbors. At the end of each chapter you will find some questions and some space for you to write down some personal application and some notes. There is also a 4 part video series that you can watch on youtube each week and take some notes here in the book as it ties in the themes from the week. Hopefully you can watch this with a small group and participate in the discussion questions together. Before the 30 days are over we're also encouraging you to engage in a Love Our City community service project. This will probably be something with your church, or your small group. If they aren't hosting any projects, it is something you could create yourself with a group of friends, co-workers, or with your family.

So you might be wondering what happened to Carlos. He didn't come back to church right away, but I kept building with him and he soon started a relationship with Christ. He has been through some ups and downs in the past couple decades, but I recently flew back to Pennsylvania and was the best man in his wedding. He and his new wife are serving Christ, involved in their local church and God is doing some great things in his life that all sparked from that basketball court back in 1993. I'm praying that you'll have some basketball court encounters over the next 30 days that will change the course of your neighbor's eternity. I'm praying that God will awaken some new things inside of your heart that will change the way you look at your city. We have a team of people praying for you and your neighbors. Let's get ready to Love Our City!

Day 1

"Our Problem"

"I know all the things you do, that you are neither hot nor cold. I wish that you were one or the other! But since you are like lukewarm water, neither hot nor cold, I will spit you out of my mouth!"
- Revelation 3:15 NLT

"The system's so foul – got us thinking we need it / Work more, spend more, but the cycle's repeated..."
– Urban D. "Appreciate" (Unorthodox Album)

We are comfortable. We are very comfortable. We live in a culture with so many options and choices. Everything is literally available right at our fingertips. We order our food, our Uber, and our new kitchen sink right from our phone as we simultaneously stream videos and scroll our social media timelines. We are over-stimulated, over-stretched and overwhelmed. We are busy in our comfort. Our vision is blurred. Hip-Hop artist Andy Mineo's Uncomfortable album warns of this epidemic as the chorus on his opening track says, "Nobody told me you could die like this, nobody told me you could die from bliss..." People are dying all around us, but we can only find the time to complain about our Wi-Fi being too slow.

Most of us want significance. We want to make a difference. Many of us want to "Love Our City", but most of us have little margin in our lives. Whatever space we have is quickly filled with trivial things that won't matter in the scope of eternity. We really want change, but we ourselves don't really want to change. In his book, Overrated, Eugene Cho drops a serious truth bomb stating, "Most people are more in love with the idea of changing the world, than actually changing the world." Ouch.

Our culture today is similar to the church in Laodicea. Jesus challenged their mindsets, allowing them to see that their lukewarm lifestyles would lead them to be spit out of his mouth. This is one of the most misquoted passages in the Bible. Revelation 3:15 reads, "I know all the things you do, that you are neither hot nor cold. I wish that you were one or the other! But since you are like lukewarm water, neither hot nor cold, I will spit you out of my mouth!" This verse is many times interpreted and preached that God wants us to be either hot or cold towards him. Be all the way in or all the way out. No half-stepping. No faking it. I've heard it preached like this multiple times. Back in the day, I believed this and even explained it like this myself. That can sound good, but that's far from the correct context.

I preached a message at my church on this passage called "The Lukewarm Bucket Challenge". At the beginning of the message, I read the verses you just read and I asked the congregation a true or false question, "These verses mean God wants you to be either hot or cold towards him? It's all or nothing. Is that statement true or false?" I brought six people up on stage to take the challenge and sat them in chairs facing the crowd. If they answered it correctly, they would get a free T-shirt, but if they answered it wrong, they would get a bucket of lukewarm water poured on their heads. It was an intense moment. Our DJ was spinning some upbeat music and the crowd was on the edge of their seats. Five out of six people got it wrong! So did we really pour a bucket of lukewarm water on people's head at a church service? I'll get to that in a minute.

The Laodiceans in Revelation chapter 3 were wealthy and comfortable, just like most of us. The city of Laodicea was located in modern day Turkey. It was a cosmopolitan city that was economically booming. They were crushing it! In fact, in 60 AD there was a huge earthquake and they refused any aid from the Roman government as they insisted they would rebuild everything with their own wealth. The people were very independent and prideful. But, even with all their money and their luxury, the Laodiceans had a problem. They were thirsty.

Have you ever been thirsty on a hot day? My daughters love to go to theme parks here in Florida. And as any good dad would do, I sometimes find myself walking through the Florida heat to wait in long lines to get on roller coasters that give you a headache. Florida summers at the theme park are a lot of fun with 95 degree temperatures combined with 95 percent humidity! Have you ever gone up to a water fountain on a scorching day like that? You are hoping for a refreshing cold mouthful of water, but instead you end up getting lukewarm water with a nasty taste and smell to it? If so, you're not alone. I've experienced this multiple times at these theme parks I love oh so much. I think they strategically do this so you have to buy a

$6 bottled water or an $8 soda, but that's another sermon for another book. Being thirsty on a hot summer day paints an interesting picture for us. None of us like lukewarm water on a day like that. However, what this meant for the church in Laodicea was on another level. It painted a much more vivid picture than us standing at a lukewarm water fountain in the heat.

Even though Laodicea was a wealthy city, they had no fresh water source of their own. A smaller city called Hierapolis, which was six miles north, was known for their hot springs. People would travel from all over the Roman Empire to bathe in the hot springs of Hierapolis. It was known to help heal people of certain illnesses. The hot water was useful for bathing, cooking and washing clothes. That hot water had a purpose. To the south of Laodicea, there was a smaller city called Colossae. Paul had planted a church there and even wrote a letter in the New Testament to them called Colossians. Their city was blessed to have these cold springs with fresh pure water for drinking.

The Laodiceans built pipelines, called aqueducts, to these cities north and south of them in order to supply fresh water to their city. Unfortunately, by the time the hot water traveled over six miles from Hierapolis to Laodicea, it was lukewarm and tasted foul due to the pipeline deposits floating in it. Similarly, when the fresh cold spring water traveled over ten miles from Colossae to Laodicea, it became lukewarm and carried a foul taste and smell.

When Jesus shares this illustration in Revelation 3 with the church of Laodicea, it carries a literal meaning as they constantly struggled with dirty lukewarm water. People would literally spit it out when they tasted it. The church of Laodicea nauseated Jesus. They make Him so sick He spit them out. The word spit in the English language does not begin to express the depth of Jesus' disgust for the church of Laodicea. The word used for "spit" in Revelation was originally written in Greek, "emeo," which means vomit!

So Jesus didn't mean I'd rather you be hot for me or cold for me... No, what He meant was, I would rather have you be useful for me. Hot water was useful. Cold water was useful. Lukewarm water was not useful for anything.

We want people to be useful for Jesus and we want to teach them how to be useful for Jesus. But pouring lukewarm water on someone's head for answering a question wrong... that would be plain wrong. When five out of six people got the question wrong regarding what Jesus meant about being Lukewarm, we came up with a plan. They were blindfolded and thought they were going to get water dumped on their head. Instead as we built the anticipation and counted down from 3, 2, 1... they got a bucket full of tiny shredded paper pieces on their heads. The crowd laughed! Their blindfolds came off and the people were relieved. A couple of the ladies didn't appreciate picking the shreds out of their hair, but at least they didn't get soaked.

The shredded paper had a real significance as an illustration. We can do a lot with a piece of paper. It can communicate a number of things as we print, or write something on it. But, when a piece of paper is shredded into thousands of little pieces it becomes useless. When we are lukewarm or too comfortable we can become useless. We can't fulfill the purpose God has for us.

Now remember, this passage of scripture wasn't written to everyone who lived in the city of Laodicea. It was a message specifically for the people in the church of Laodicea. If we're being honest, this letter could have easily been written to the people in the church of America today. So many people go to church, but overall they are not living out their spiritual purposes. They are not allowing themselves to be useful for God to work in them and through them; And Jesus makes it very clear that those kinds of people make him sick.

Love Lesson:

God doesn't want us to be hot (all in) or cold (all out), he wants us to be useful! (Rev. 3:15)

Love Question:

In what ways would you say that you are currently useful for God?

Love Application:

How can you apply this to your life?

Love Notes:

What stuck out to you? What else is God saying to you?

Day 2

"Our Wealth"

"You say, 'I am rich. I have everything I want. I don't need a thing.' And you don't realize that you are wretched and miserable and poor and blind and naked."
- Revelation 3:17 NLT

"I'll be honest, it was hard at first / Even though we say we want to put God first / Because we all struggle with this material thirst / But we can't take nothing when we get in the hearse"
- Urban D. "Give, Multiply, Grow, Repeat" (Love Our City Album)

Yesterday we talked about our comfort and looked at Revelation 3 where Jesus was stressing that He wanted us to be useful for Him. But, there's more! Jesus says additional things to the church in Laodicea that also line up with us. Verse 17 shows us that the people who were extremely wealthy claimed that they didn't need anything from anyone. Even when a big earthquake hit them, they refused any aid from the Roman Government. It was because they had this prideful vibe of "We got this!" But Jesus tells them that they are oblivious to the fact that spiritually they are pitiful, blind, and homeless. They were living in deception. They thought they were something that they were not.

Have you ever met someone like that? There once was a lady who came up to her pastor and told him, "I have a sin and I need your help. I come to church every Sunday and I can't help thinking I'm the prettiest girl in the congregation. I know I shouldn't think like that. I want you to help me conqueror this sin." The pastor looked at her and smiled and said, "Child, don't worry about it, in your case it's not a sin, it's just a horrible mistake." Many of us have some funny stories of people living in deception. But at the end of the day, there are so many people that think they are good and that "they got this", but the reality is that they are the total opposite. Similarly, the people of Laodicea thought they were all good, but they weren't.

Most of you reading this are living in the richest country in the world today. America is the richest and most advanced civilization in the history of mankind. I know most of us don't feel rich, but we are. We are filthy rich! I'm not talking some religious talk about being spiritually rich. I'm talking about real deal cash money rich. We don't feel this way as we live in a hyper consumer culture, which is always pushing on us something new to buy, to experience or to eat. But let me break down some facts. One in three human beings live on less than two dollars a day - that's 2.4 billion people. If you check out the website www.globalrichlist.com you can see where you rank. I'm actually a member of the 1% club. I couldn't believe it, but according to their data, I'm up there in the top richest people on the planet. Now before you think I'm balling out selling tons of books and music... let me share this stat; According to the U.S. department of Health and Human Services, the poverty level for a family of four was $24,600 [1]. Guess where that lands on the list? The top 2.09%! Even if you are in poverty in the United States you are still near the very top compared to people in other parts of the world. According to the Bureau of Labor Statistics, the median wage for workers in the United States in the fourth quarter of 2017 was $44,564 for a forty-hour week [2]. That puts the average person in the United States in the top .42%. We may not go around saying, "we are rich" like the Laodiceans did, but on a global scale we are very rich. Most of us are actually richer than they were and have access to cleaner water than they did.

Jesus gave the Laodiceans a prescription to go from self-reliance to total dependence on God. Jesus told them they needed to buy three things. They couldn't go to the bougie Beverly Hills Mall of Laodicea and they couldn't get it from Amazon Prime. They could only get it directly from Jesus. In verse 18, Jesus says,

"I advise you to buy gold from me,
gold that has been purified by fire. Then you will be rich."

Laodicea was one of the richest cities in ancient history. Many people could afford to buy anything they wanted. But, here God is saying that they needed spiritual riches through faith in Christ. He talks about gold that has been purified by fire. Earthly riches that we have will burn up, but spiritual wealth has eternal value, that's why the last part of the verse says, "then you will be rich." Jesus then tells them the second thing to buy from him is white garments. Those white garments represent spiritual purity. One of the biggest sources of wealth in Laodicea were garments. Their specialty was black wool cloth. This was their signature product that made them rich and famous in the Roman Empire. Their prosperity was also due to their well-known eye ointment.

People came from all over the region to get treated at their famous eye clinic and school. So here is Jesus making this analogy that they need to get this third thing from him -buy eye ointment for your eyes so you will be able to see. This spiritual eye ointment would help them open up their eyes to their sin so they would see truth and ask God for forgiveness.

Even though thousands of years and thousands of miles separate us from the Laodiceans, we have a lot more in common than we think. Most of us have access to buy whatever we want right from our smartphones. Because of their wealth, the Laodiceans had whatever luxuries of their day available. Although we may not feel rich, we are extremely wealthy compared with the rest of the world. But, the material things we have will get old, worn out, and eventually go out of style.

Jesus said where your treasure is there your heart will be also. So, we have to ask ourselves: What are we constantly working towards? What is the treasure we are going after? If we are honest, our main focus isn't always working on our spiritual wealth. Many of us are thinking about financial wealth, bills we are trying to pay off, a vacation we are saving for, a new toy we want, or something we need to buy the kids. The list seems to never end. I know this firsthand as a husband and father of two teenage daughters. It's easy to forget how blessed we are and to forget about our responsibility to use it in ways to have eternal impact.

> *"Abundance isn't God's provision for me to live in luxury. It's his provision for me to help others live. God entrusts me with his money not to build my kingdom on earth, but to build his kingdom in heaven." - Randy Alcorn*

Love Lesson:

We are much richer than we think.
Where much is given, much is required.

Love Question:

How could we be more eternally productive with the wealth that we have?

Love Application:

How can you apply this to your life?

Love Notes:

What stuck out to you? What else is God saying to you?

Pastor Tommy & Michael Clayton
(Former NFL Player for TB Bucs & NY Giants)

Day 3

"Our New Prescription"

"I correct and discipline everyone I love.
So be diligent and turn from your indifference."
- Revelation 3:19 NLT

"Our soul lives on after we leave this earth / And the Bible promises
heaven to those who have a spiritual rebirth / With Jesus /
He comforts us – He frees us / So the best is yet to come – it's gonna
get better / I'll see you soon fam – cuz we're gonna live forever!"
- Urban D. "Eternal" (Love Our City album)

need to regularly remind myself, and my girls that all these earthly things are just temporary, but the spiritual things are eternal. And I'm a Pastor! But I know I'm not alone in this. We can all struggle with our vision at times. God gives us a prescription for our lenses, just like he gave the Laodiceans a prescription in this passage. We know this prescription is good for us. We know it will help us see clearly. We know it will help us avoid all kinds of headaches. However, we think the non-prescription sunglasses that the culture offers are cooler. They are constantly advertised to us and it seems like other people wearing them are having an amazing time. So we end up putting them on most of the time to fit in. It seems so normal. From time to time, we'll put on our God prescribed lenses when we go to church, in front of our parents, and in front of other Christians we want to impress. The truth is, wearing them occasionally doesn't correct the real direction of our vision.

God has been rocking me lately about eternity. I recently lost my father. His life and his ministry touched countless people who were changed forever. I am so grateful for his example and I know he is with the Lord. He was sick for close to seventeen years, so his passing was closure for our family; nonetheless, it is still super hard to lose your dad. On top of that, as I am writing this chapter I am at my mother's house taking care of her in her very last days of her battle with cancer. It has been extremely difficult to watch her decline physically and mentally. My mom was always the life of the party and made friends everywhere she went. She loved people and she loved to talk. When she was healthy, saying goodbye was always a challenge on the phone because she just kept going and going. The last few months, I consider myself lucky just to keep her on the phone for four or five minutes because she has lost most of her energy. I've cried many tears and I'm sure there will be a lot more coming, but what I do have is hope. The Bible consistently presents hope as a confident expectation about what is going to happen in the future. Hope is one of our deepest virtues as Christians. We are supposed to be hopeful people. We should find joy in hope, boast in hope, hold strong to our hope, overflow with hope, and even defend our hope. We go through trials because trials produce character, which in turn produces hope. People in our communities are desperate for hope. We are supposed to be hope pushers!

What is the object of our hope? God! We hope in God because of who he is, what he has done and what he is going to do in the future. In **Titus 1:1-2**, Paul told Titus,

"Paul, a servant of God and an apostle of Jesus Christ to further the faith of God's elect and their knowledge of the truth that leads to godliness - in the hope of eternal life, which God, who does not lie, promised before the beginning of time."

In **Acts 24:14-15**, Paul was defending himself before Felix in Caesarea and said,

"But I admit that I follow the Way, which they call a cult. I worship the God of our ancestors, and I firmly believe the Jewish law and everything written in the prophets. I have the same hope in God that these men have, that he will raise both the righteous and unrighteous."

Paul even said in Corinthians that if there was no resurrection of Christ, we were all hopeless. Creation longs to be freed from its bondage to corruption and futility. If you sit and watch the news, you are reminded of how messed up our world is from ISIS, to North Korea, to corrupt politicians, to the murder count in Chicago. It seems hopeless. Christ followers look forward to a new heaven and a new earth where we are in the presence of God. This is our blessed hope. This is the hope that causes us to Love Our City.

My mother passed away on September 8th, 2017. Even though I watched my mother's health rapidly deteriorate, I was hopeful. I know that she had a relationship with Christ and I am confident she got a new body that cancer could never invade. Her suffering and her pain are now over, but I miss her like crazy. I am human and I am grieving. I can't believe she is gone. There are times I'm ready to pick up the phone and call her about something and then reality sets in that I can't do that anymore. Even through all my pain, I am still hopeful. I keep reminding myself that everything here on earth is just temporary. God is strengthening my eternal perspective.

As an artist, one of the ways I deal with pain is by creating. I wrote a spoken word piece about losing my mom and my dad in the same year. I have written hundreds of songs and it is by far the most emotional one I have ever penned. It passionately shares my pain, my perspective, and my hope. We created a music video for "Eternal" and it has touched tens of thousands of people. Additionally, I also launched a clothing line called "Eternal" that has the tag line "Live Forever" (**www.eternal.clothing**). My hope is not in my temporary time here on this sin-sick planet. My hope is ignited in my eternal perspective when I think about how we will live forever in God's presence in a place without sorrow, pain, or death.

We can correct our vision problem if we change our lens, lean in and focus on the bigger picture. We know everything here is temporary, but if we can learn to operate and prioritize from this perspective it will change the game. We can't take any of our material things with us. The only thing we can take with us into the next life is people. For the last few months that my mom was alive, there was a parade of people coming to visit her: neighbors, friends from work, friends from church, and friends from out of town. My Facebook feed was filled with so many comments from people sharing about what my mom meant to them. My mother was always full of hope and positivity. She loved God and loved people. She loved her city.

What mark will you leave behind after you breath your last breath? Will you be known as someone who loved your stuff or someone who loved people?

"At the end of the day people won't remember what you said or did, they will remember how you made them feel."
- Maya Angelou

Love Lesson:

The only thing we can take with us to heaven is people.

Love Question:
How are you trying to bring people with you to heaven?

Love Application:
How can you apply this to your life?

Love Notes:
What stuck out to you? What else is God saying to you?

Day 4

"Our Cities"

"Yes, I try to find common ground with everyone,
doing everything I can to save some."
- 1 Corinthians 9:22b NLT

"Imagine a new life, a new fam, a new city / Imagine a place with no
political committee / Just lots of love, daps and high fives /
Romans 6:4 in action – living new lives"
- Urban D. "New Life, New Fam, New City (ReBuild album)

We live in an era of unprecedented human mobility. Our cities and metropolitan areas are rapidly changing and growing at a pace like never before. The share of the world's population living in urban areas increased from just 3 percent in 1800 to 14 percent in 1900. By 1950 it reached 30 percent. Today, this number stands at more than 54 percent [1]. More and more people are clustering in metropolitan areas and there is evidence that this trend will continue. The United Nations and the International Organization for migration both estimated that around 3 million people move to cities every week [2]. That is close to 430,000 people every day-nearly 18,000 every hour. The global urban population is expected to double to 6.4 billion by 2050, representing 70% of the world's population [3]. Our cities are not just quickly growing they are also becoming more and more diverse in age, ethnicity, culture and class. All these different worlds are converging in our cities. One single block could represent four generations, with over a dozen languages spoken with million dollar condos on one side of the street and section eight housing on the other.

Realtor.com shared that their data indicated Baby Boomers are moving back to cities. Instead of migrating south to retirement communities in Florida or Arizona they are moving back to metro areas they abandoned when they started raising families [4]. At the same time another substantial demographic moving into cities are rich, young, childless, educated, and white. In addition cities continue to be a magnet for immigrants and undocumented immigrants. Time. com reported that the majority of America's undocumented immigrants live in twenty urban areas with New York being the largest with 1.15 million [5]. These three demographics that are continuing to mix into cities are adding new layers to the melting pot.

Although the white population is moving back into the cities at rates we haven't seen in decades, they are no longer the majority. According to the US Consensus the white people made up 53% of people in cities in 1990. By 2010 that number dropped to 41%. Meanwhile the Hispanic population during that same period of time grew from 17% up to 26% and the Asian population grew from 5% to 8%. Surprising the African American population also fell in cities from 24% to 22%. We could easily think that more white people moved to the suburbs. But, the suburbs have also grown much more diverse as well. In 1990 white people made up 81% of the suburban population, but this dropped to 65% by 2010. The Hispanic, Asian, and African American populations all grew substantially in the suburbs during this same time period. We can see that metropolitan areas as a whole are becoming more and more diverse. 2014 was the first year that more than 50% of children under the age of five were minorities. Many school districts in metropolitan areas are now becoming majority minority (students are non-white) [6].

This is a huge opportunity for Christ-followers, but yet a huge challenge for many of them and the churches they are a part of. The days of going to a church where everyone looks like you are quickly fading. Not just in our cities, but the suburbs as well. A mono-ethnic church doesn't make sense in much of our current reality and it certainly doesn't in our future. It's estimated that over 80% of churches are declining or stagnant [7]. There is obviously a disconnect between these churches and their communities. We cannot approach outreach and evangelism the same way we did decades ago when things were less diverse.

Every city is different. I have the opportunity to travel regularly to different places to speak, train, and consult. I see lots of similarities and differences in each city. Every city has some neighborhoods that are defined by race or certain ethnic groups. But many cities have more and more neighborhoods that are becoming more diverse. I've lived in Tampa, Florida for over twenty years and although there are some areas that are more defined by ethnicity, many areas of the city and suburbs are diverse. Surprisingly, some of Tampa's suburban neighborhoods are actually even more diverse than other parts of the city. Here is a story from a pastor friend of mine that leads a church in our rapidly changing suburbs.

Brad White | *Founder and Lead Pastor - LifePoint Church*

My family had the privilege of moving to Tampa, Florida in August of 2000, and planted LifePoint Church in October of the same year. What drew us to this northeastern part of our city was that it looked like us. When we started the church and for the first five years it was filled with people who were Anglo. Over the next few years we began to notice a shift in our culture and in LifePoint with more and more diversity. The demographic studies we looked at were confirming what we were seeing with our eyes. The world was moving to Tampa, and we needed to shift our thinking and strategy. As Leaders we sensed that this was a move of God and we wanted to respond accordingly. How incredible is it that God would bring the nations to the streets where we live and work. We began to reach out to churches that were known for diversity both locally and nationally and asked for wisdom. This opened our eyes to realities that had never crossed our minds. We learned about how different cultures see and experience church. We began to pray and seek Gods help in contextualizing what we were learning.

Our first move was to intentionally increase the diversity on stage. This showed people that we were open to change and riding the wave that God was sending. The second was to diversify our leadership, so we began to look through a much broader scope of candidates for positions. Third, we began to tell the stories from the stage and through media of people from different races and ethnicities. Fourth (we are in the middle of this step), is to teach our people how to see the world differently and to seek to connect with people different than them. If we are going to reach people who come from countries where they have heard little or nothing of Jesus, we must be willing to leave our comfort zone. Fifth, we realized we needed to adjust our worship style (which has primarily been an Anglo style all these years). This change is slower, because for us it takes time to find the people that can do it differently. We believe that very soon our worship will be more of a Mosaic of songs and styles to help connect people from all over the world to our Savior King. All of these steps need to be reviewed and addressed regularly because our nature is to slip into a pattern of what we know and what comes easy. Embracing diversity is hard work, but it is worth it. God has allowed us to reach people and see many people turn to Jesus as their Savior that we would not have reached had we been unwilling to change. We've had families leave over the last few years because they wanted more of a homogenous church, but I wouldn't trade where God is taking us for anything in the world. What we have experienced in our city is becoming more and more common, so lead with your eyes and ears open! Heaven will be diverse and when we embrace it as Christian leaders, we can get a taste of Heaven on Earth.

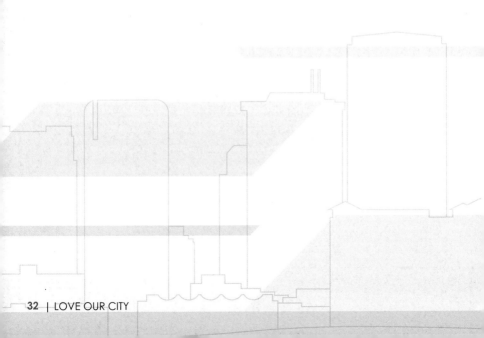

Love Lesson:

Our cities and suburbs are becoming more diverse in age, culture, class and ethnicity.

Love Question:

In what ways have you noticed your city changing?

Love Application:

How can you apply this to your life?

Love Notes:

What stuck out to you? What else is God saying to you?

Day 5

"Our Crossover Rebuild"

"But now I said to them, 'You know very well what trouble we are in.
Jerusalem lies in ruins, and its gates have been destroyed by fire.
Let us rebuild the wall of Jerusalem and end this disgrace."
- **Nehemiah 2:17 NLT**

"Rebuilding can knock the wind out of us / Kinda like a sucker punch
hits straight to your gut / Nehemiah – had the physical rubble /
Plus the spiritual rubble / Plus the outside opposition and trouble /
Shallow breaths on the double / Trust me... I had more than a couple"
- **Urban D. "Breathing Room" (ReBuild Album)**

I n 2010, the church I lead relocated to an abandoned Toys R' Us building on Fowler Avenue and retrofitted a 43,000 square foot building. The area of North Tampa was nicknamed "Suitcase City" due to its high eviction rate, homelessness and transient nature. Fowler Avenue was dotted with lots of vacant retail and restaurant buildings that once had thrived. The great recession hit our city hard and many businesses that survived were fleeing to the new mall and retail areas that were opening in the suburbs. This was a forgotten part of the city. It was risky to invest over a million dollars in an old retail box and put a church there. But, we knew God wanted us to rebuild this community and bring the love of Christ. I share the details of the miracle story of our church getting in the building in my previous book "Rebuild". We made it our goal to rebuild the neighborhood on the Nehemiah model: physically, spiritually, emotionally and economically.

We had this vision that the neighborhood would look different in five years and much different in ten years as we rebuilt it. This seemed like a lofty goal considering the stats. Shortly after we moved in the University Area Community Development Corporation did a massive survey in our zip code and found the unemployment rate to be over 25%. The rental rate for housing was at 94%. Crime was over 100 times higher than other parts of the city. It looked bleak.

Loving a transient community is not easy. We ministered to many families, discipled them and helped them get stable... and then they moved away. Then there were some that had a poverty mentality where they didn't want to do anything to change their situation, but they would gladly take whatever you were offering for free. Others didn't want to take anything, as they didn't trust anyone. Loving your city takes time. Building a reputation takes time. Seeing real results takes time. But, five years into it we were seeing some solid change. We had planted a lot of seeds and they were beginning to grow. Thousands of people had started a relationship with Jesus at our outreaches and church services. We baptized our 1,000th person.

(Fun Fact: We baptized actor/rapper Christopher "Play" Martin from Kid N' Play the day we hit 1,000 baptisms!) There were hundreds of families touched through our mentoring programs and discipleship classes. The spiritual landscape was being impacted. People were moving forward as they experienced the love of Christ and began loving on others around them.

In 2015 there were some big physical shifts that began to happen in our neighborhood. It was designated an innovation district. Although there are rough neighborhoods, it also includes the University of South Florida with close to 50,000 students, several research hospitals, the second largest VA hospital in the country and several other large anchor businesses. Just a few miles east of the church, the district includes the Busch Gardens theme park, which attracts millions of tourists each year. The anchor tenants got together with the city, county and business community and started a district to revitalize the area as it had such a bad reputation. I kept reading about it in the newspaper and online. I wanted to meet these people. I knew there was potential to work together to rebuild my city.

In April of 2016, Crossover Church was invited to some meetings by an outside firm that was studying our community to provide recommendations for its revitalization. We were invited to the meeting as they considered us an anchor tenant and they wanted our input.

We were the only church sitting at the table of about twenty major community businesses and institutions.

At the meeting I met Mark Sharpe, the director of the Innovation District (The !p) and former county commissioner. Mark and I immediately hit it off. We met at the church a few weeks later and he invited me to be on the Advisory Board of the Innovation District, one that is filled with CEO's and business leaders. Others had to financially contribute to be on the board, but Mark said he wanted me involved because I understood the community and would help shape the way the board would invest its resources in neighborhood redevelopment. I was humbled, honored and thankful for the invitation. It was a fulfillment of the rebuilding plan that God had put on our hearts many years before. In 2017, I was voted to become vice-chair of the board specifically over community engagement.

We are watching our neighborhood change before our eyes. Unemployment has dropped. The eight-lane road that our church sits on now has very few vacancies. There is a new Starbucks a block away that replaced an abandoned gas station. Several new stores and restaurants have been built. New apartments are being built for student housing and residents. The mall two blocks away is about to undergo a one billion dollar redevelopment. It will be turned into a mixed-use city center called "Uptown". The Innovation Alliance (The !p) received a $3.8 million dollar Federal Tech-hire grant to train 1,000 low income young adults in the tech and medical fields and get them job certifications. This is going to be a game changer for so many families. We don't want gentrification to push people out, but create new opportunities for our current residents to be part of the rebuild. There is so much work to be done, but we are seeing progress. Our church is involved in the inner workings of this community transformation, as we have loved our city for so many years. We've built trust and credibility to sit at the table. We believe the best is yet to come!

Love Lesson:

Loving your city takes time. Building a reputation takes time. Seeing real results takes time. People are worth it!

Love Question:

How is your church involved in your community? What are new ways you could influence culture around you?

Love Application:

How can you apply this to your life?

Love Notes:

What stuck out to you? What else is God saying to you?

Baptism of Christopher "Play" Martin (Kid N' Play)

Day 6

"Our Harvest"

"So pray to the Lord who is in charge of the harvest;
ask him to send more workers into his fields."
- Matthew 9:38 NLT

"We've been empowered, so we empower others / Fathers and
Mothers / Sisters and brothers / Haters and lovers / The haters - they
love us / Once they discover the hope that we cover – we see /
There's no blindness / We loving our city with acts of that kindness"
- Urban D. "Love Our City" (Love Our City album)

When most Christ-followers think about missions they think about going to a third world country on a "missions trip". Evangelical Christianity in the West has traditionally focused more on "the ends of the earth" than on "Jerusalem." Many Christ-followers find it easier to go somewhere foreign and "love a city", than to go somewhere familiar and "love their city". But this is changing, as Millennials want to serve more and more in their own backyards. They see the need in front of them and they want to engage and be hands on.

In Matthew chapter 9, Jesus sees the needs in front of him, but he sees them with different eyes than his disciples. The scripture tells us that Jesus felt deep compassion for them. He saw their physical needs and even healed many of them from diseases and illnesses. Even greater, he saw their spiritual needs. Jesus used the metaphor that the people were like sheep lost without a shepherd. Then he switches metaphors and says the harvest is great, but the workers are few. The harvest and the workers show God's "need" met by man: God uses people to minister to other people.

God planted you in the city where you live now. It's your Jerusalem. Many of you may not originally be from there, but that is where you are now. Legendary Hip-Hop artist Rakim wrote a classic lyric that resonates with this; "It ain't where you're from its where you're at!" (1) Most of my childhood was spent growing up in the Philadelphia area. I loved my city. I loved the sports teams, the culture, the music, the graffiti, the soft pretzels and of course the greasy cheese steaks. I had family, friends and a close church family. There was a lot of history, roots and deep relationships. Back in the day I would have told you I would live in Philly for the rest of my life. But, sometimes God has totally different plans for us and he transplants us elsewhere. I've now been in Tampa, Florida for over two decades. Tampa is my home. My community. My people. Tampa is my responsibility. My family is invested here and my church has deep roots in our city. You have to choose to bloom where God has planted you... or transplanted you.

Tampa would not have been my first choice, but now that I've been entrenched in it for so many years, I'm so grateful God brought me here. I love my city.

Our harvest is all around us in our own cities. There are people that are ripe to respond to the gospel, but there are not enough people living it out and sharing it in a credible way that connects. Jesus said pray for more workers for the harvest. If we begin to seek God and pray, many times we'll find out we are part of the solution to reach that ripe harvest right down the block. The Greek word kairos means "opportunity", "season", or "fitting time". In Jesus' day an appointed time was expressed as kairos. The New Testament refers to eighty-six kairos opportunities. Jesus gave a very specific prayer request as he instructed the church to pray during a kairos moment. This prayer request in Matthew 9 came after Jesus healed a man with leprosy, a Roman's soldier's servant, spoke truth about the Kingdom of Heaven, healed Peter's mother in law, calmed a storm, cast demons out, healed a paralyzed man and had dinner with a tax collector that the Pharisees referred to as scum. Did I mention he also raised a dead girl back to life? So you can see that Jesus was pretty busy. In that moment he looked out into a crowd of people and he sees a great need and he calls his people to action. He sees opportunities, he sees potential, he sees unfinished stories, but he sees a problem with this kairos moment as well.

How do you look at your life's story? The culture tells us - It's your life. You own it. You keep it. You do whatever you want but yet, the scripture tells us - My life is part of God's big story. My story is part of this community, my family and my church. God is writing my story. When we write our own story, chances are we end up writing from some of our own hurt, pain and bad experiences. When you allow God to write your story he can take all of our kairos moments (the good, the bad, the ugly and the beautiful) and turn them into an unbelievable best seller. So when Jesus looked out into this field he saw some New York Times best selling autobiographies. He saw an incredible harvest.

Love Lesson:

The harvest is local, regional and global (Acts 1:8)

Love Question:

What is the spiritual condition of your city?
What does the harvest look like?

Love Application:

How can you apply this to your life?

Love Notes:

What stuck out to you? What else is God saying to you?

Day 7

"Our Disruption"

"Your love for one another will prove to the world that you are my disciples."
- John 13:35 NLT

"Dreadlocks, fades and fitteds / A multi-cultural faith community that's committed / To the great commandment and the great commission / We orthodox in our beliefs – but not in our fishing"
- Urban D. "Un.orthodox" (Un.orthodox Album)

There are many churches that are declining, dwindling, and dying as they refuse to make necessary changes as culture and demographics around them rapidly shift. But, in the midst of the bad news, there are several bright spots where churches are engaging their changing communities. They are reaching the harvest and seeing true church growth and revitalization as they learn to create new paths of ministry.

These are some amazing stories from some friends that have learned to adapt to the disruption. As we learn to love our cities in new ways this could become our finest hour!

Ken Claytor | Founder and Lead Pastor – Alive Church

The goal was simple. To have a church that "resembles heaven". Or so I thought. I remember living outside of Washington, DC when God first called us to Gainesville, Florida. I didn't know much about Gainesville. In fact I had to Google it to figure out where it was after the Lord spoke it. However, the one thing I did know for sure, is that we were going to build a multi racial church. But, I didn't know how challenging that would be to accomplish as a young black man. I remember in the beginning of our ministry. There was a lady that asked my wife so gently, is it ok, If "I" was to come to your church. She said of course we would love for "you" to come. Completely naïve at the moment, we had no idea that she was concerned about coming because she was…"white".

It has always amazed me that whites and blacks and everyone in between can work together in corporate America Monday thru Friday, pass the football together all day on Saturday, but Sunday morning is the most segregated time of our week. We had to do something about this. We wanted our church to "resemble heaven". At the time we were 98% black in attendance but our city was 23%

black. We tried it all. We said we were a church for "all people". We invited in white guests speakers. We photo shopped pictures to market our church as being diverse. It worked to get them in the door. But, unfortunately most wouldn't stay.

What did we do? I am glad you asked. Ultimately it is the favor and grace of God. There were several things combined that we did that caused this change but the major one was that we decided to be very intentional. We decided that our church would "resemble heaven" no matter what the costs. That means that we became intentional about who is on stage, who is on our website, who is on our videos, who is at first impression points of our church. We needed to make sure that new guests felt like "They belonged". Our music reflects that intentionality. We had to make sure that our music wasn't to black or too white. We had to find an in-between that all could enjoy. Our staff reflects that. We could not have a staff that was off pace with the demographics of our city. If we are going to win our city we need our staff and leadership to reflect the demographics of our city. Some might say that that seems fleshy. The truth is the exact opposite in our eyes. We naturally go to people who look like us, talk like us, and have our same characteristics. However there is power in diversity. We learn so much more and grow so much more when we get out of our bubble. However diversity does not happen by accident. It doesn't matter how much we pray. It only happens when we take God's love and we become intentional about who we want to reach and going out of our way to make them feel like they belong.

As a black pastor, I didn't have many models to learn from. This was 10 years of trial and error. I saw a lot of white pastors with multi cultural churches, but not a lot of black leaders. Our call and our assignment was to have a church that looks like heaven and reflects our city. We are learning everyday, but are well on our way. John 13:35 that states, "By this everyone will know that you are my disciples, if you love one another". Our church is now about 60/40 in diversity and growing more diverse every Sunday. We have made leaps and bounds in a short two years and now see all different races, and classes and cultures worshiping God together and not just that, but literally doing life together as family. Racism is not just a natural problem. It is a spiritual problem. The devil would love for us to stay divided. A kingdom divided against itself can never stand. My prayer is that the world will begin to look to the church for answers on racial reconciliation. Racism has never been a skin issue. It has always been a sin issue. God's love is the key.

David Crosby, D.Min | **Founder and Lead Pastor - Community Church**

My wife, Bekah, and I planted Community Church fifteen years ago in the heart of the beautiful Pocono Mountains, Pennsylvania. Historically known as a resort community, the Poconos has more recently become a bedroom community to northern New Jersey and New York since it is located only 68 miles from Manhattan. Over thirty thousand people commute an hour and a half one way from the Poconos into New York City and New Jersey every day. The Poconos became the fastest growing community in Pennsylvania for over 10 years in the late 1980s and 1990s with thousands of "transplants" moving from the city into the mountains. This has created a new community geographic definition known as post-rural – a rural community comprised of both rural and city people.

Of course, this reality has had a great impact on the culture of Community Church. I describe Community Church this way: if the hit television show "Duck Dynasty" got together with the hit show, "The Housewives of New Jersey" – and they had a baby – that would be our church. It's a beautiful collection of both rednecks and city slickers. Take one look in our lobby and you would see a lot of stilettoes and camouflage walking around. In fact, we now have over 40 nations represented in our church without one dominant ethnic culture. It's a beautiful living picture of what heaven will look like one day with every tongue and tribe on earth worshiping together community.

When starting Community Church, we honestly had no specific intention of planting a multicultural church. We simply had an abiding love for people and the desire to build a "whosoever" church. The Bible says, "For whosoever shall call upon the name of the Lord shall be saved." (Romans 10:13 KJV) However, we quickly began to realize that our church was ethnically diverse, with three predominant people groups: African Americans, Whites and Hispanics. One weekend about a year or so into the church plant it occurred to me as I stood stage of the high school auditorium where our portable church got its start that I was the only white person standing on the stage. I found myself surrounded by a Jamaican, a Trinidadian, a Guyanese and a Puerto Rican and yet another white Italian man from Brooklyn – but Brooklyn counts as its own country in my book. If you ever had the pleasure of knowing someone from Brooklyn you would agree.

Leading a multicultural congregation is the future of the church in America. It's been my long held belief that your congregation should be a mirror reflection of the community in which it's located. So if you live in a diverse community you should worship in a diverse church. Racial reconciliation and social justice are central to the Gospel. Jesus himself stood for inclusivity over exclusivity. We see this when he entered the temple where the money changers had set up shop in the outer Gentile court. Jesus famously turned over the tables and threw out the money changers, not just because they were exploiting the poor but because they had pushed out an entire people group from worshipping in the presence of God - the Gentiles. That's why he said in that moment, " "Is it not written: 'My house will be called a house of prayer for all nations'? (Mark 11:17) Jesus' house is for all nations. If Jesus were a Puerto Rican he would've said it this way, "Mi casa es su casa." My house is your house.

Love Lesson:

Although many churches are declining and dying, there are also several that are growing and thriving as they learn to adapt to the changes in their communities.

Love Question:
What story resonated with you and why?

Love Application:
How can you apply this to your life?

Love Notes:
What stuck out to you? What else is God saying to you?

Watch the video at www.youtube.com/urband813

*"'You must love the Lord your God with all your heart, all your soul, and all your mind.' This is the first and greatest commandment. A second is equally important: 'Love your neighbor as yourself.' The entire law and all the demands of the prophets are based on these two commandments." - **Matthew 22:37-40 NLT***

We all have some PROBLEMS...

1. We have a ____Business~~Comfort~~____ Problem.

"Therefore, go and make disciples of all the nations, baptizing them in the name of the Father and the Son and the Holy Spirit. Teach these new disciples to obey all the commands I have given you. And be sure of this: I am with you always, even to the end of the age."
- Matthew 28:19-20 NLT

* They were ___Empowered___ by the Holy Spirit and He helped them get past their comfort issues.

* When we step out of our comfort zone God can empower us in ___Supernatural___ ways to reach our neighbors.

2. We have a ___Comfort___ Problem.

3. We have a ___~~Vision~~ disruption___ Problem.

Discussion Questions

1. How busy are you on a scale of 1-10?
   (1 being not busy and 10 being very busy).

   1   2   3   4   5   6   7   8   9   10

2. What are some things that keep you so busy that it can be challenging to put God first and love your neighbor?

3. How can applying "Love your neighbor as you love yourself" take you out of your comfort zone?

Peter was previously very uncomfortable to admit he even knew Jesus. Now he was able to stand up and preach to thousands.

Read Acts 2:14-41

4. Have you ever had God use you in a supernatural way?

5. What neighbors are difficult to see in a positive way?

6. What things do you see rapidly changing around you (getting disrupted)?

7. How could you, your small group and your church respond to the disruption and reach people in creative new ways in your city?

Day 8

"Our Sons, Students and Partners"

"Their responsibility is to equip God's people to do his work and build up the church, the body of Christ."
- Ephesians 4:12 NLT

"We live in a culture where it's all about the individuals / Forget about the principles / It's all about residuals / It's opposite of Philippians 2:3 / Where Paul says I need to think about you – before I think about me"
- Urban D. "Empowering Others" (ReBuild Album)

Jesus regularly faced all kinds of accusations. He was accused of blasphemy, low morals, ungodliness and even being on the same team as Satan. This didn't stop Jesus. It didn't distract Jesus. He stayed focused. He ignored the unfair criticism and was about his father's business. Even though people were talking junk about Jesus he still stayed on his mission. He kept loving people. Our job is to love others without stopping to ask whether or not they are worthy. When Jesus looked out at the people he was moved with compassion. The Greek word that was used for compassion in Matthew chapter 9 was the strongest word for pity in the Greek language. It describes the compassion that moves a man to the deepest depths of his being. It was to be moved as to one's bowels (the bowels were thought to be the seat of love and pity). Yes, they took it there!

The problem with this compassionate kairos moment was that the harvest was plentiful, but the workers were few. Back in Jesus' day there were an estimated 170 million people in the world [1]. Today, our world population increases by 228,000 people every day [2]. We now have over seven billion people on the planet. The harvest is more plentiful than ever. I see how great the harvest is where I live in Tampa. My city was the 5th fastest growing metro area in the United States in 2016 adding 58,000 new people to our population of over 3 million [3]. A lot of people moving to my city are looking for new opportunities like I was when I moved here from Philly. Some people are running away from something else. Many of them don't have roots here. They don't have family, history or traditions here. They don't have many relationships. Most importantly, many of them don't have a relationship with Christ. A few years ago Tampabay.com reported that only 34.7% of people in Tampa regularly go to church. That was the second lowest city outside of Seattle. More people went to church in Las Vegas aka Sin City than in Tampa [4] (they were #3 on the list). When I take the focus off of myself and look through the eyes of Christ my heart is heavy with compassion for my city.

I would guess that you also have a great harvest in your city and not enough people to work it. It can seem overwhelming at times. There are so many people with so many needs. Where do we start? Jesus gave us a great starting point in Matthew 9:38 where he says, "So pray to the Lord who is in charge of the harvest; ask him to send more workers into his fields." We have to start with prayer. In this whole passage of scripture there is only one command that Jesus gives us. It is to pray. We need to pray to God that he will send more workers into the fields to reap the harvest. But, we can't just sit back and only pray. Some people will only pray that God will send more pastors and missionaries out into the harvest. Yes, we need more pastors and missionaries, but all of us are called to be missionaries in our local harvest. We have to get out there in the fields and also train up others to join us. God uses pastors, teachers and church leaders to equip the entire church to do ministry. Ephesians 4:12 stresses this as it says, "Their responsibility is to equip God's people to do his work and build up the church, the body of Christ."

After Jesus gave this prayer request in Matthew 9:38, in the next chapter we see Jesus call his disciples together and send them out to do ministry. He gives them instructions and empowers them to go and do what he has done. When Jesus first met these guys several of them were grimy fishermen from the neighborhood that had a lot of rough edges. They didn't seem like ministry material. They didn't fit the typical description of workers for the harvest. But, Jesus handpicked these guys, discipled them over time and then empowered them. This is the model. We can't reach the harvest on our own. We must reach people, disciple them, and empower them to go and do what we are doing. We can see how Paul also followed this model in scripture as he met his spiritual son Timothy in Lystra in Acts 16. He saw something in him and took him under his wing. Paul became his spiritual father. He called Timothy his "true son in the faith". Young Timothy went on tour with Paul from town to town and observed and assisted. Timothy became a student. Some of Paul's very last words were written to Timothy as he wrote him two letters and was giving him some final instructions as he was empowering him to pastor the church he started in Ephesus. Paul said something very unique in Romans 16:21. He called Timothy his fellow worker and his partner. So Timothy was a son who became a student who then became a partner. This is the model as we reach the harvest and raise up others to reach our cities.

I met Benny Fernandez III in the lobby after a church service about five years ago. You couldn't miss him, as he is 6'3, 300+ pounds with a platinum grill (teeth) and tats on his arms and neck. I noticed him a few times in service, but he always slipped out before I could meet him. But one Sunday I finally caught him and said what's up to him. He shared that he was from the neighborhood and his family owned a body shop around the corner with a Martial Arts studio on the second floor. I told him I knew where it was and he told me to stop by sometime. He didn't think I would ever stop by, but I did that week. I rolled up and caught him working under a car in the shop. He was both happy and shocked to see me. Benny put down his tools and took me into the office and started to open up about his life. His family had this business for decades, but also previously had a big drug business in the neighborhood. They opened up the Martial Arts studio to give back to the neighborhood. All the classes they offered were free. Benny admitted he was still struggling in many areas of his life, but was trying to get on track. He loved our church and really wanted to get involved. I immediately saw potential in Benny. I knew he could make a serious impact in our city. I committed in my heart to build with him and disciple him. I'd love to tell you it was a fast process, but it wasn't. Benny would come around for a few weeks and then disappear for a few months.

I passed by his shop everyday on my way to work and I would pray for him and his family. I would regularly stop by and talk with him and pray with him. He would tell me, "I'll be at church on Sunday Pastor T", but he didn't show up. I took him out to lunch several times and talked with him, encouraged him and challenged him. He would express his desire to change and get on point. Benny would make promises about seeking God, getting involved at the church and being accountable. He would come around again for a few weeks and then disappear even longer. This was a process that continued for a few years. He was struggling with drugs, women, anger, baby mama drama, family issues, and more. I'll share the miracle that happened with Benny in the next chapter. As I close out today's reading I want to stress that there will be moments when you are reaching out to the harvest and it seems literally impossible. So many people are so broken and have so much baggage that it seems like they will never get it together. But we have to remember that we are not the Lord of the harvest, we are just the workers. God uses us as the workers, but he ultimately is the one that changes their hearts.

Love Lesson:

Our job is to love others without stopping to ask whether or not they are worthy.

Love Question:

Do you have a spiritual son or daughter that you are raising up to be a student and eventually a partner?

Love Application:

How can you apply this to your life?

Love Notes:

What stuck out to you? What else is God saying to you?

Day 9

"Our Differences Aren't Barriers"

*"Teach these new disciples to obey all the commands
I have given you. And be sure of this:
I am with you always, even to the end of the age."*
- Matthew 28:20 NLT

*"We're all equal, we're all the same / Christ's blood was
for the Black, the White, the Jew, the Gentile, the free, the slave /
Let's squash all the stereotypes in Jesus name"*
- Urban D. "Skintone" (The Missin' Element album)

It takes time for spiritual sons and daughters to become students and eventually partners in ministry. I saw potential in Benny and adopted him as a spiritual son, but the first couple of years he was still out there in the streets. Then out of nowhere, something began to change in his heart. Benny started showing up every Sunday, he was coming to every Bible study, and he was even coming to the men's events. He wasn't just showing up, he had this hungry look of fire in his eyes. His breakthrough was happening! The true Lord of the harvest was moving in his life. On April 3rd of 2016 I had the privilege of baptizing him and a few weeks later I had the honor to officiate his wedding. That year he also started going to Bible College at our church to go into ministry. This former drug dealer was now studying to be a pastor. I made him go to my friend Chris Cambas for Christian Counseling and pre-marital counseling to work through some of his issues. Chris soon also adopted him like a son and even hired him part time that eventually turned into full time. Benny shared with me that he really wanted to share his story with other drug addicts. He began calling some drug intake centers around the city to see if he could come in and talk to the people in their program. He got turned down at several places and began to get discouraged. Finally a program director agreed to meet with him and hear his story. The director was blown away by his story and his presence. She knew he could connect with the men in the program, so she scheduled him to come and speak to the entire facility. Benny was excited, but suddenly nervous as there were going to be over one hundred and twenty men at the session. I encouraged him and prayed with him on the phone the day he went to the program to speak.

A few days later Benny came to my house and read me a letter that expressed the details of his story and how he came to Christ. He wrote it for one of his classes in Bible College, but he also felt compelled to read it to the men in the program. It rocked the men in the program as it had most of them in tears. He wanted me to hear it. As we sat at my kitchen table we were soon both in tears as well. They were tears of joy. My tears had an additional layer to them when he read, "I have involved myself in a church that feels like a home. I have never felt this way about a church. The pastor is like a brother to me.

I hope to start things in the church for people struggling with drugs."
I had been praying for over ten years for someone from our church
to rise up and lead a ministry to reach out to people with addictions
and brokenness. God confirmed in that moment that the person I was
praying for was Benny Fernandez. I soon took Benny to a Celebrate
Recovery meeting at my friend's church. The leader took Benny under
his wing and began to mentor him and walk him through the CR
steps to become certified. He even took Benny to a CR conference in
another state. God was piecing together each step to reap a huge
harvest in our city. Fast forward to June 16th, 2017. It was the official
launch of Crossover Church's Celebrate Recovery "Friday Night Live".

Like Paul and Timothy's relationship, Benny went from my
spiritual son, to my student, to my ministry partner. He is now a ministry
leader at the church. He preaches and leads groups every Friday
night. Our Celebrate Recovery quickly became the largest in the city
as many people from our church starting attending and we partnered
with the local Salvation Army. They bring a couple buses full of men
and women in their recovery programs. Benny has been empowered
to reach a whole segment of the harvest that I can't. Benny went from
being the neighborhood dope pusher to his new nickname "The Hope
Pusher". We must raise up those we reach in the harvest to become
fellow partners in working the harvest.

Some of Jesus' last words pointed to the harvest. Matthew
28:19 Jesus told his disciples to "Therefore, go and make disciples of
all nations, baptizing them in the name of the Father and the Son and
the Holy Spirit. Teach these new disciples to obey all the commands I
have given you. And be sure of this: I am with you always, even to the
end of the age." These verses are full of action. They are full of verbs.
We see the words go, make, baptize, teach and obey. Jesus didn't tell
us to just sit around and hope that people will change. Jesus gets us
directly involved in helping people change. He uses people to reap
the harvest. But, what does that harvest look like? People read this and
get excited about making disciples. But, many times we miss the part
that says make disciples of "all nations". Many churches may send out

missionaries or a mission team to other nations, but we are also called to make disciples of all nations right here in our cities. That means people in our cities that are from a different tribe than you. They may be from a different ethnic group. They may be from a different culture. They may be from a different economic bracket. They may be from a different background.

There were many things about Benny's background that were different than mine. He is Cuban and was raised in a heavy drug-dealing environment. He experienced all kinds of physical and verbal abuse and he struggled with severe drug addiction for over eight years. That wasn't my story. I couldn't personally relate to several things he had gone through. But, that didn't stop me from being able to love him and disciple him. I never looked at any of those things as barriers. I never judged him or looked at him in an inferior way. I looked at him as a brother that was made in the image of God. God connected us in many ways that we could relate and do life together. Never be afraid to reach someone different than you.

I poured into him and taught him the ways of God that I've learned and applied to my own life. There can be discipleship moments where we feel unqualified. We don't know what to say. We don't know what to do. We may not have experienced some of the things they went through. They are asking you questions you don't have the answers to. They are telling you things they have gone through and you are trying to keep a straight face, as you are shocked. The very last line of Matthew 28:20 is the best part. Jesus promises, "I am with you always." We are not alone in reaching the harvest. We are not alone in raising them up to work along side of us and reach the harvest. He is right there with us to give us exactly what we need exactly when we need it.

Love Lesson:

God can use us to reach people that are different than us.

Love Question:

Are there people around you who are different than you that you falsely believe you can't reach?

Love Application:

How can you apply this to your life?

Love Notes:

What stuck out to you? What else is God saying to you?

Montell Jordan & Kristin Jordan speaking at Crossover

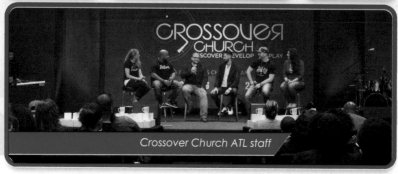

Crossover Church ATL staff

Day 10

"Our Neighbor"

"The man answered, 'You must love the Lord your God with all your heart, all your soul and all your strength, and all your mind.' And, 'Love your neighbor as you love yourself.'"
- Luke 10:27 NLT

"Illadelph – where I grew up with cons and fakes / Philly Cheesesteaks / A place where hip-hop bakes"
- Urban D. "Roots" (Un.heard album)

There was a religious leader who stepped to Jesus and tried to antagonize him and justify himself at the same time. This guy knew the Mosaic Law inside and out. He asked Jesus, "Teacher, what should I do to inherit eternal life?" Jesus replied in classic form and answered with a question. Actually two questions! He said, "What does the law of Moses say? How do you read it?" The religious leader answered, "You must love the Lord your God with all your heart, all your soul, all your strength and all your mind. And Love your neighbor as you love yourself." Jesus agreed and told him, "Right! Do this and you will live." So that part of the conversation went well, but here is where it gets interesting. Luke 10:29 tells us, "The man wanted to justify his actions, so he asked Jesus, 'And who is my neighbor?'"

This religious leader was basically trying to choose who he would love and who he could cross off of his neighbor list. He was looking for a loophole. He wanted to just love people that looked like him, were from the same income bracket and lived in the same neighborhood. You know... the same tribe. Unfortunately a lot of people still operate like this. A lot of Christians and a lot of churches operate like this. Many of them may not even do it with full intentionality... it's just what is naturally more comfortable. In Day 1 we talked about our comfort problem. But, if you look at this word neighbor, there isn't a loophole. It literally means your neighbors - those who you live around, work around and play around... aka your city! In the Greek language it means "someone who is near." The people near us in our cities are not just one ethnic group, one age demographic, one class or one culture - they are diverse.

When our church does Love Our City week and regular outreach events we always have people asking us, "Why are you doing this?" Their surprised actions are funny, but also sad. They can't believe this diverse group of people is giving something away and showing love with no strings attached. Who does that? Apparently, almost no one nowadays! The media regularly shows up at our events and asks us the same question, "Why are you doing this?" Our response is that we take the words of Jesus seriously. He told us to love our neighbors as we love ourselves. We are putting that into action. We care about our neighbors and we are striving to make our city a better place. They are blown away.

What did Jesus say to this guy in Luke chapter 10 that was looking for a loophole? Jesus replied with a story about a priest, a religious guy and a Samaritan. It almost sounds like the beginning of a joke, right? But it was no joke! In verse 30 Jesus said, "A Jewish man was traveling from Jerusalem down to Jericho, and he was attacked by bandits. They stripped him of his clothes, beat him up and left him half dead beside the road. By chance a priest came along, but when he saw the man lying there, he crossed to the other side of the road and passed by." What? The priest just passed him by? If anyone should have helped him I would have thought it would be the priest. He's a pastor, a shepherd, and spiritual leader. Maybe he was in a hurry? It was a seventeen-mile journey between Jerusalem and Jericho and maybe it was about to get dark. He also may have been worried that it was a trap that if he stopped and helped the guy he might have been jumped too. I don't know. I'm trying to give him the benefit of the doubt, but it still seems a little messed up.

Jesus continued the story and said, "A temple assistant walked over and looked at him lying there, but he also passed on the other side of the road." So this second religious man stopped and looked at him, but he decided to keep going as well. Wow, we're zero for two and they were both leaders from the church. Not a good look! But now here is where it really gets interesting. This third guy comes rolling up in verse 33. Jesus said, "Then a despised Samaritan came along, and when he saw the man he had compassion on him." Did you catch that? What kind of Samaritan? Despised. But wait, most of us probably heard about the Samaritan before and it wasn't the story of the despised Samaritan... it was the Good Samaritan! What's up with that? If you don't know the historical context you can miss the punchline.

Jesus highlights this Samaritan as the good guy, but in their culture the Samaritans were always known as the bad guys. There was no such thing as a Good Samaritan. You had these two religious dudes walk right by the half dead man on the side of the road, but you have this Samaritan come up and have real compassion. The man that was hurt was Jewish. Samaritans were considered a totally different ethnic group, as they were only part Jewish. They intermarried with foreigners and adopted some of their idolatrous customs. They were considered half-breeds and universally despised by Jews. Samaria was also a place of refuge for Jewish people that were criminals running from the Jewish authorities. If Jews were traveling from Jerusalem to Judea the shortest way was to go directly north and pass through Samaria to get there. But, they were known to go east and cross the Jordan river and then go north and bypass Samaria, then go west and cross the Jordan river again to get to Judea. This added an additional twenty-five miles to their trip. They didn't want to pass through Samaritan towns, drink from their wells or have any contact with them. As you can see, there was a lot of drama between the Samaritans and the Jews.

The Samaritans were outsiders. They were misfits. They were considered to be second-class citizens. But, Jesus shares this story of the Samaritan looking at this hurt Jew as his neighbor. He was a human that was made in the image of God. Even though this hurt Jew probably hated Samaritans and would have despised him if he were well, the Samaritan still showed him love. Look at what happened next. "Going over to him, the Samaritan soothed his wounds with olive oil and wine and bandaged them. Then he put the man on his own donkey and took him to an inn, where he took care of him. The next day he handed the innkeeper two silver coins, telling him, 'Take care of this man. If his bill runs higher than this, I'll pay you the next time I'm here.' Then Jesus asked him, 'Now which of these three would you say was a neighbor to the man that was attacked by bandits?' The man replied, 'The one who showed him mercy.' Then Jesus said, 'Yes, now go and do the same.'"

The Samaritan was the surprise hero of this story. It wasn't the priest. It wasn't the Levite. It was the despised half-breed. Jesus is drawing a strong contrast between those who knew the law and those who actually followed the law in their lifestyle and action. Jesus gives this example of someone unexpected being a good neighbor and said now you go and do the same. There's no loophole. If a Samaritan can show love to someone who literally hates him, than you can too! If we're honest, many of us can relate to that religious leader that asked Jesus 'Who is my neighbor?' There are times when we don't feel like getting out of our comfort zone. We would rather hang around people that are more like us. We would rather show love to people that we know will show love back to us. But God puts people in our paths for a reason. It may be that homeless person who smells and is mentally unstable. It may be someone of a different skin color or age. It may be someone who is Muslim wearing a Hijab. When we see these differences it can sometimes cause us to look the other way or think that we can't reach them. Many times we are the exact person that God wants to use in that moment.

Love Lesson:

There is no loophole in the command to love your neighbor.

Love Question:

Why did Jesus use a "Despised" Samaritan as the surprise hero of the story in Luke 10?

Love Application:

How can you apply this to your life?

Love Notes:

What stuck out to you? What else is God saying to you?

Day 11

"Our Thirst"

"Jesus replied, 'Anyone who drinks this water will soon become thirsty again. But those who drink the water I give will never be thirsty again. It becomes a fresh, bubbling spring within them giving them eternal life.'"
- John 4:13-14 NLT

"The American Dream / It's not all that it seems /
From the ghetto to Wall Street – it's money making schemes /
From suits and ties – to Tims and Jeans /
Most just need to be redeemed"
-Urban D. "The American Dream" (The Immigrant album)

We don't love our neighbor to earn God's love. We love our neighbor as an expression of what God has already done for us. God loved us first, even when we were in the middle of our dirt. He loved us when we didn't deserve it. He loved us when we didn't expect it. He pursued us. Now, we get the opportunity to do this for others. We reach out to people in the middle of their junk, even if they don't deserve it. They may be ungrateful and be in the middle of a mess that they created. They might have a bad attitude and get nasty with us. But, don't catch amnesia. Many of us were like this during a season of our lives and God used someone to pursue us and show us love, right when we needed it. Let's pursue our neighbors and love them with no strings attached. The Samaritan loved this beat up Jew on the side of the road. He was a hot mess. He may not have even been grateful as a despised Samaritan was helping him. The Samaritan still loved him, cleaned him up and paid for his hotel room with no strings attached. This not only impacted that hurt man, but it is still impacting us today as we read about it and ponder the application to our lives.

With God's help we must learn to shift our attitude towards our neighbors, especially the ones that give us attitude. There are three attitudes displayed in this story Jesus told in Luke 10, The Robbers attitude was "What's yours is mine and I'm going to take it." The Priest and the Levite's attitude was "What's mine is mine and I'm going to keep it." The Samaritan's attitude was "What's mine is yours and I'm going to share it." Which attitude is yours today? Dr. Martin Luther King Jr. preached from this story in Luke the night before he was killed. The sermon was called "I've been to the mountaintop". Dr. King pointed out that the priest and the Levite didn't stop to help the man because in essence they asked themselves the question, "If I stop to help, what will happen to me?" But, the Samaritan asked a much different question: "If I don't stop, what will happen to him?" Are we really concerned what happens to our neighbors?

We live in a world where everyone is thirsty. They are looking for happiness, peace, contentment, purpose and pleasure. They are trying to find it in all kinds of ways. I had a season of my life where I tried to quench my thirst with material things, girls, and popularity, but at the end of the day I was left even more thirsty. I was drinking from the wrong well. Many of our neighbors are drinking from the wrong well with poisonous water. And poison makes us sick... and sick people do what? They make other people sick, just like hurt people - hurt people. Broken people - break people. But, on the flip side, forgiven people - forgive people, healed people - heal people and loved people - love people. So, there is hope and healing available, even if you've gone through some deep issues. Hurt and abuse are complex subjects. There can be lots of layers; sexually, verbally, physically and emotionally. With all the people reading this I realize there are many holding this book in their hands that have been abused. As a pastor and spiritual leader I want to say I'm so sorry for what you've gone through. I acknowledge your hurt and pain. I want to let you know that you matter! It makes me angry that you had to go through that, that is why I felt this needed to be included in a book about loving other people. Some of us still have some big holes and big wounds. It's hard to love when you leak. Even if you haven't gone through hurt personally, you know someone that has. God wants to use this book to equip all of us to help restore people as we follow the example of Jesus.

In the gospel of John Chapter 4 we see another story about an unlikely neighbor. Jesus met a Samaritan Woman at a well. This happened because Jesus was actually traveling through Samaria with his disciples. Instead of going the normal Jewish bypass route that was twenty-five miles out of the way, he took the less-preferred route directly through Samaria. Jesus asked her for a drink of water. She was shocked and expressed it to him, as men normally didn't speak to women in public and even greater than that He was a Jew and she was a Samaritan. Jesus replied, "If you only knew the gift God has for you and who you are speaking to, you would ask me, and I would give you living water." She still didn't understand as she stated that Jesus didn't have a bucket and that she didn't think he could offer better water than Jacob's well had. Jesus then told her, "Anyone who drinks this water will soon become thirsty again. But those who drink the water I give will never be thirsty again. It becomes a fresh, bubbling spring within them, giving them eternal life." This Samaritan woman was thirsty and this caught her attention. She asked Jesus to please give her some of this incredible sounding water, she was tired of having to come to get water at this well. That's when Jesus asked her to go and get her husband. She told him that she didn't have a husband. Then Jesus read her email and told her that she previously had five different husbands and she was currently living with a man that she wasn't married to. She admitted he was right.

This woman had a tough life. There may have been abuse; sexual, verbal or physical. She was done with marriage, as the man she was with now was not her husband. She was thirsty. She had been through a lot of pain and a lot of loss. All of us have experienced some drought seasons, which can leave us dry. But there is living water that can eternally quench our thirst. Jesus makes it available to us so we can share it with our neighbors.

"You are a product of your past, but you're not a prisoner of it. You can change." - Rick Warren

Love Lesson:

We don't love our neighbor to earn God's love. We love our neighbor as an expression of what God has already done for us.

Love Question:

We are all thirsty... so what well (what you watch and listen to) are you regularly drinking from?

Love Application:

How can you apply this to your life?

Love Notes:

What stuck out to you? What else is God saying to you?

Day 12

"Our #metoo World"

"Then Jesus told her, 'I am the Messiah!'"
- John 4:26 NLT

"I wonder how she cope / It's been weeks since she's seen a bar of soap / Addicted to dope / The oxymoro is her name means hope (esperanza)"
- Urban D. "Broken English" (The Immigrant album)

The #metoo movement spread viral at the end of 2017 and into 2018. Several well-known activists, celebrities, and actors started using the hashtag and shared their stories of abuse and hurt which they had hidden for years. Soon there were millions of people joining in to post up their personal stories. Our church did a four-week #metoo series with conversations about what the Bible says about abuse and hurt. We also addressed church hurt. It was an amazing month that helped so many people confront hurt and begin the healing process.

The World Health Organization estimates that 1/3 of women worldwide get abused [1]. The Washington Post said 54% of American women had unwanted and inappropriate sexual advances at work [2]. Stats in this article show that in the majority of cases people don't report it, as they are ashamed, afraid of what people think, intimidated that they may lose their job, or they think that no real action will take place.

Time Magazine's person of the year for 2017 was the "Silence Breakers" - the voices that launched the #metoo movement. They called the #metoo movement the fastest social change we've seen in decades [3]. It took a lot of courage for women and men to come forward and tell the stories of harassment and assault. We've seen countless people exposed and many of them famous people. It's good that justice is taking place. The interesting part is that there is morality behind this movement. It's fighting for justice and morality in a world that has been going the other direction for so long. There has been an agenda that produces media and entertainment that constantly pushes a sexually charged message. It promotes us to sleep around with everyone, be sexually free, porn is good, porn is normal, open marriages and open relationships are fine. People are now beginning to wake up and realize that type of message backfires, that agenda backfires, that lifestyle backfires. People are thirsty and people get hurt.

Sometimes we're so messed up that we feel that we can't approach God. But as we take a deeper look at this Samaritan Woman in John chapter 4, we can see Jesus' example. From a Jewish perspective she had three strikes against her, but that still didn't stop Jesus from ministering to her. First, she was a woman. In their social customs men didn't talk to women in public. It was even rare that a husband talked to his wife in public. Second, she was a Samaritan. Jews avoided Samaritans. They didn't want to walk through their towns, drink from their wells, eat their food or have any contact with them. There was this bitter hatred between the two groups. The third strike we see is that she had five husbands. We don't know exactly what happened, but now she was living with some man that was not her husband. She had some issues, some hurt, some pain, quite possibly even some #metoo abuse. She also was at the well at noon. Women normally came to the well early in the morning or later in the day in groups. But, perhaps because of her public shame she came to the well alone when nobody else was around. So why would Jesus talk to this woman who was a despised Samaritan that was sleeping with some guy that wasn't her husband? Because Jesus didn't come for the healthy people, he came for the people that were sick. He came for those who had problems. He came for those who have a #metoo story... he came to bring healing and hope!

That's good news, because every 98 seconds someone is sexually assaulted in America [4]. Not just women, but 1 out of every 6 men has been sexually abused [5]. People are thirsty. They are drinking from the wrong well. They get sick and they make other people sick. Most perpetrators that abuse people were abused themselves. So how do we find healing? Jesus offered this living water. The Samaritan woman thought Jesus was talking about flowing water, but he was talking about salvation from sin's bondage and condemnation. Water can temporarily satisfy our thirst, but salvation permanently satisfies our soul.

Jesus always raised the value of women. There were several times in the gospels we see where he did this. He defended them, listened to them, forgave them and healed them. After this Samaritan woman leaves Jesus (who just confronted her about her past and her current situation), she goes back to town and tells everyone, "Hey come see this man who just told me everything I ever did." She wasn't coming with shame, but with dignity. Jesus knows what you've done. He knows what I've done. He knows what we've been through. He knows the pain we've experienced. He knows some of the shame you might be holding. He told the woman at the well that he was the messiah. He came to save us. We all need a savior. He has living water for us and our neighbors.

We must use discernment as we are reaching out to love our neighbors as so many of them have also been hurt. Many of them have walls up. They have layers of issues, years of pain and some have generations of dysfunction. Not everyone has grown up like you. We all have our own unique set of experiences, values and privileges. People aren't looking for clichés or quick answers. We must learn to listen and acknowledge their pain and frustrations. Jesus is our Messiah and our Savior and he loves those with a #metoo story and we should too.

"The scriptures make it clear that we are called to forgive our neighbors that harm us. But forgiving them does not require giving them the same level of access to our lives. When someone continues to abuse us, we are wise to put boundaries in place. Forgiveness never requires submission to continued abuse." - Lucy Kyllonen

Love Lesson:

He came for those who have a #metoo story... he came to bring healing and hope!

Love Question:

Have you recently listened to someone's #metoo story? How can you help them find healing and hope?

Love Application:

How can you apply this to your life?

Love Notes:

What stuck out to you? What else is God saying to you?

Day 13

"Our BEST R.O.I."

*"Look, I am coming soon, bringing my reward
with me to repay all people according to their deeds."*
- Revelation 22:12 NLT

*"Because you can't take nothing when you leave this planet /
It's all about faith - that's the way that he planned it /
I'll stay true, keep rockin' microphones and flowing /
Cuz I know up above my inheritance is growing"*
- Urban D. "Endurance" (The Missin' Element album)

We are great at wasting things. If you live in America, we are some of the biggest wasters in the world. We lead the world in food waste as we throw away 150,000 tons of food every day [1]. We only make up 5% of the world's population, but we use 24% of the world's energy [2]. Many of us waste our resources, our time, our talent, and even our lives! Loving our neighbor is never a waste of time, talent or resources. Jesus told us that even if we give a cup of cold water in his name we will be rewarded. He will remember our labor of love. The scripture tells us to store up our treasures in heaven. Everything here is temporary, but in a million years from now we'll still be in heaven. Yet, most of us are only focused on storing up treasures here. We're investing here in the things we think will bring us the biggest ROI (Return on Investment). As I'm writing this, the stock market is breaking new records, real estate prices are rising, cryptocurrency and Bitcoin prices seem to have everyone talking. People are dreaming how they can make the right investment moves that could change their life. I'll admit, it can be easy to get caught up in this as I've watched some people I know make a lot of money in investments recently. But, in the big picture it is all just temporary. If I could pay my house off that would be great, but in one hundred years from now it won't matter much, as I won't be here.

The things that are really going to have the greatest ROI are eternal investments. We can't take any of our stuff with us. Someone else will be living in my house and my cars, clothes and technology will all be obsolete. The only things we can really take into eternity are people. If we invest in our neighbor's lives and they start a relationship with Christ, then we will see them again in eternity. The Bible talks about rewards in heaven. The concept of this is illustrated in the New Testament teaching by the use of the Greek word in Matthew 16:27 that is translated as "reward". This word literally means a paycheck. This eternal compensation that we are to receive is not some free gift, but it's an actual payback for the work that was done for God. Revelation 22:12 says something very similar where Jesus says, "I am coming soon, bringing my reward with me to repay all people according to their deeds." I like the way the Message Translation says it, "Yes, I'm on the way! I'll be there soon! I'm bringing my payroll with me. I'll pay all people in full for their life's work."

So all of us have an account in heaven where our permanent net worth is being increased by our life's work for God; our deeds, our giving, our love. Whatever we accumulate here is just temporary net worth, but we increase our permanent net worth when we follow the words of Jesus and we love our neighbor. Jesus shares he is preparing an amazing place for us. We can dream and imagine that it is going to be incredible, but there is some mystery to it as I think there should be. What if we could see what we were going to get? Did you ever think about that? What if we could go to heaven.com and type in our user name and password and we could see how our treasures in heaven were looking? What if we could watch our permanent net worth rise? So the next day you might bring your neighbor to church, pray for someone at work and feed some homeless people on the way home... only to see how your investment grew. So you log into heaven.com and you can see that your house went from a 3 bedroom to a 5 bedroom. You see where I'm going with this? What would we do then? We would go out and love our neighbors more than ever so we could see our investment increasing. For many of us it would probably become addicting in a not so good way. Our motives could become selfish and self-centered and we would miss the things God wants to genuinely do in us and through us. So, keep in mind there are incredible rewards in store for us when we serve God's purposes here on earth, but stay focused on the task at hand.

Jesus wants his church to find ways to build bridges with our neighbors and show them the love of Christ in real and tangible ways. He wants us to love people who are different than us. They may not actually live in our neighborhoods, but they work there or shop there. They are present in our city. We need to find ways to engage them and demonstrate unconditional love. So here is our application for this chapter: we can all be better neighbors! Biblical love transcends boundaries of geography, race, religion, socio-economic status, and even convenience. Loving our city is not just a project, an event or even a week of serving. It's should be all day, every day 24/7.

Love Lesson:

*Our earthly net worth is temporary,
but our heavenly net worth is permanent.*

Love Question:

*What are some things that you can do to increase your heavenly
net worth and cause you to "store up treasures in heaven?"*

Love Application:

How can you apply this to your life?

Love Notes:

What stuck out to you? What else is God saying to you?

Day 14

"Ourselves"

"And you must love the Lord your God with all your heart,
all your soul, all your mind, and all your strength.
The second is equally important: 'Love your neighbor as yourself.
No other commandment is greater than these."
- Mark 12:30-31 NLT

"We need to love our neighbor as we love ourselves /
Empower other people – focus less on self /
Shift our eyes away from the wealth / And truly rebuild
with the spiritual health"
- Urban D. "Empowering Others (ReBuild album)

Jesus told us the second most important commandment is to "Love our neighbor as we love ourselves." Some of us may think the problem isn't learning to love our neighbor, but it is learning to love ourselves. A lot of us have issues with ourselves. We can think before we can "Love Our City", our neighbors, our spouses, our kids and our friends... we need to first learn to better love ourselves. This is how we can intend to initially read into this passage. I've read into it this way myself. I regularly see a lot of people that are messed up, have a poor self-image, and regularly make choices that hurt themselves. But that's not what Jesus is speaking of in these verses.

Jesus is saying that we start with this human trait of loving ourselves. All of us have a powerful instinct of self-preservation and self-fulfillment. We want to be happy and satisfied. We strive for it. We fight for it. We want food for ourselves, things for ourselves, a place to live for ourselves. We want our lives to be significant. We want to matter. All of that is self-love. You could boil it down to a deep longing to diminish pain and to increase happiness. This is a human trait that is hard wired into all of us. It causes us to move forward and function each day. It is not a bad thing, but it is not always manifested in a healthy way.

Even in our selfishness, we are still fighting for ourselves. Even if we are in survival mode or in a really unhealthy place, at the root, we are trying to protect ourselves. So Jesus is talking about this thing inside of us that we don't have to learn. It's already built in us. To hunger for food is not evil. To want to be warm in the winter is not evil. To want to be healthy is not evil. So this human trait is not evil in itself. If it has become evil in your life that will become evident in how you respond to Jesus' command of "love your neighbor as you love yourself". So just like you feed yourself when you get hungry, will you feed your hungry neighbor when they need it? Just like you work to live in a comfortable place, do you desire that for your neighbor? As you seek to be safe from violence, do you seek security for your neighbor? As you look for friends yourself, are you being a friend to your neighbor? As you are striving to advance in your career, will you help your neighbor advance in theirs? In other words make your self-seeking equal to your self-giving.

The big word in the command "Love your neighbor as you love yourself" is not just "love". Everyone's thoughts immediately move to the word "love". But, the challenging word here is actually "as". So if you are innovative and entrepreneurial in pursuing your own happiness and building your dream, be just as innovative for your neighbor's dreams. If you are passionate and over the top about your family, but just as passionate that your neighbor will have a healthy family. Wow. If we really take Jesus at his words here, that is pretty intense. "As ourselves" is pretty deep as we love us some us. It can seem overwhelming and not humanly possible. That is why it important to take this statement in full context. We need the first commandment to be able to fulfill the second commandment. Remember the first commandment is "Love the Lord your God with all your heart and with all your soul and with all your mind." The first commandment is the basis for the second one. The second commandment is the visible expression of the first commandment. Before you are self-seeking or self-giving of love, you have to first put God in that number one spot of receiving your love.

When we truly learn to apply the first commandment to our lives we will find true satisfaction and love. Our self-love solely focused on ourselves will leave us empty and confused. God says, come to me, and I will give you fullness of joy. Our lives are then transformed and we have this joy that is spilling out of us. This is when we start loving ourselves in a healthy and balanced way. I could have spent a lot of time in this short chapter giving information about how to learn to love ourselves better. We all know there are a lot of people that love themselves in a very narcissistic way. There are already tons of self-help books and materials out there. But, to keep it simple, if you put God first and love him with all your heart, soul and mind then you will have a healthy heart, soul and mind. You'll love yourself properly and that will put you in a position to live out the second command. It comes more natural as we now have proper self-love that can be the content of our neighbor-love.

Remember that Jesus gave himself for the world. He gave his life for us even though we didn't deserve it or earn it. Even though we were still unclean sinners, he died for us because he loved us so much. Jesus is sharing these commands with a Jewish audience. The Jews were God's chosen people and some of them felt like they had the market cornered on God's affection. They felt like they were superior. Jesus was also saying love even the neighbor that you think is unclean. Love them like they are clean. We may not walk around thinking we are superior, but there may be some people around us that we would consider unclean. I'm not just talking about someone that is physically dirty. It may be that person with the vulgar mouth at work or school. It may be that friend that is always negative and complaining. It may be your crazy uncle that always says inappropriate things. Every family has a crazy uncle. Whether we think it consciously or subconsciously there are people around us we may consider unclean. We exclude them from the list of people that we could love as much as we love ourselves. It's hard. This is where the transforming power of Christ works on our hearts. This is a process when we upgrade our everyday lenses so we can see all people through the eyes of Christ.

Love Lesson:

The second commandment is the visible expression of following the first commandment.

Love Question:

Is there anyone I struggle with loving "as" much as I would love myself? Why? How can I work on this?

Love Application:

How can you apply this to your life?

Love Notes:

What stuck out to you? What else is God saying to you?

Watch the video at www.youtube.com/urband813

We are called to ___*bless*___ our neighbor, but many times our neighbor can end up being a ___*blessing*___ to us.

Many people ___*know*___ the truth and even ___*preach*___ the truth, but don't always ___*live*___ the truth.

*"Then a despised Samaritan came along, and when he saw the man he felt compassion for him. Going over to him the Samaritan soothed his wounds with olive oil and wine and bandaged them. Then he put the man on his own donkey and took him to an inn, where he took care of him." - **Luke 10:33-34 NLT***

Jesus switched the image of the Samaritan from ___*despised*___ to ___*good*___. He flipped the script and made the Samaritan the hero of the story.

Jesus was ___*against*___ racism and discrimination.

The Gospel is not exclusive it's ___*inclusive*___.

Paul's model was he reached people that became his spiritual sons, that transitioned into becoming his students and then eventually they became his ___*partners*___ in ministry.

Discussion Questions

1. Have you ever blessed someone in some way and it ended up being more of a blessing for you than it did for them? What happened?

Read Luke 10:25-37

2. Have you ever been in such a hurry that you missed an opportunity to help a neighbor?

3. Have you ever judged someone and had a bad impression of them, but once you got to know them they were a great person?

4. Have you experienced racism or discrimination?

5. Who is the person or people that were instrumental in helping you grow in your relationship with Christ?

6. Do you have anyone in your life that would fit in that role of a spiritual son or daughter, a student or a partner? If not... who could that be?

Day 15

"Our Leader"

"But among you it will be different. Whoever wants to be a leader among you must be your servant."
- Matthew 20:26 NLT

"Whether you're young or you're old, single or married /
The way that you Display (serve) might be varied /
At home or a work, even at church /
Come on family —we gotta put in work!"
- Urban D. "Life in 3D" (Amnesia EP)

We live in a culture that is generally self-serving. The higher you climb up the corporate ladder, the more perks you have and the more people are there to serve you and take care of your needs. We see celebrities walk around with their entourage that handle every little detail of their lives. This has been the model for thousands of years. Many people think this is the definition of success. But Jesus set a new example as he turned this idea upside down. In the gospels, there were several times where the disciples argued about who was the greatest. They wanted the perks and the attention. They wanted the shine. Jesus regularly put them in their place and let them know that is the way the world operates, but it will be different among us. Then he said something that was extremely counter cultural, "Whoever wants to be a leader among you, must be your servant."

Jesus didn't just say it, but there were actions to back it up. Throughout his ministry he served people and sacrificed many conveniences of everyday life. He was basically couch surfing staying at different people's homes as they traveled from city to city. Jesus poured out and had many long days of teaching, traveling, and meeting people's needs. He was constantly giving of himself. His disciples saw this firsthand as they were right there with him. For some reason it still didn't click for most of them at first. But one of the things that personally impacted them in a huge way was when he washed their feet. Washing someone's feet in Jewish culture was for someone at the very bottom of the ladder. The disciples regularly argued with each other about who was the greatest. They didn't want to wash each other's feet, as whoever did it first would then be admitting they weren't the greatest. But their leader - the miracle worker, healer and famous teacher took his robe off, tied it around his waste and bent down washed their nasty feet. He set the example. It was a groundbreaking moment. Loud mouthed Peter protested and told Jesus he would never let Him wash his feet. He didn't think it was proper as Jesus was his master. But Jesus told him if He didn't that he wouldn't belong to him. Peter quickly obliged.

After Jesus washed His disciples feet He put his robe back on and said this in John 13:12-15, "Do you understand what I was doing? You call me 'Teacher' and 'Lord,' and you are right, because that's what I am. And since I, your Lord and Teacher, have washed your feet, you ought to wash each other's feet. I have given you an example to follow. Do as I have done to you." If our leader and savior can bend down and wash feet, then we must be ready to roll up our sleeves and get dirty as well.

Throughout the gospels we can see how Jesus set the tone of reaching out to the lost, the forgotten and the unwanted: the woman at the well, tax collectors, lepers, the demon-possessed, prostitutes and even dirty fishermen. He told stories that made despised Samaritans the heroes and went places that most religious leaders of his day would never step foot in. If Jesus was here today he would be reaching out to all kinds of lost people in our communities: the corrupt businessmen, the strippers, the drug dealers, the gang members, the atheist college students, the prescription drug addicts, and even the Muslim woman wearing a hijab. Jesus set the pace and we need to follow his lead.

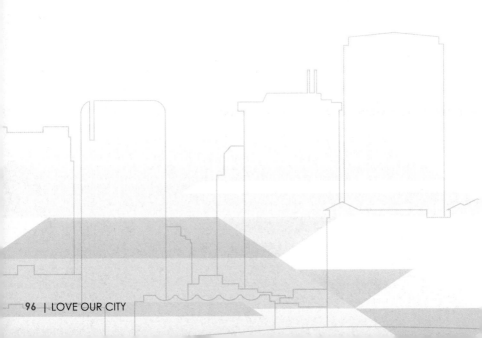

Love Lesson:

If you want to be a real leader, you must become a real servant.

Love Question:
What is a recent way you have served someone?

Love Application:
How can you apply this to your life?

Love Notes:
What stuck out to you? What else is God saying to you?

Day 16

"Our Example"

"I tell you, her sins – and they are many – have been forgiven, so she has shown me much love. But a person who is forgiven little shows only little love."
- Luke 7:47 NLT

*"There's no substitution for this thing called love /
But Christ was our substitution when he shed his blood /
There's a whole flood / Of descriptions through the scriptures /
That define agape so you won't get it twisted"*
- Urban D. "Love Revolution" (Un.heard album)

One of my favorite passages in the scripture is Luke chapter 7 where Jesus was invited to go to a religious leader's house for dinner. Now, this wasn't just any casual dinner, this was a special dinner party. Hospitality was a big deal in their culture. They had several different customs that they offered to guests. If you think about it, we also have some cultural customs in the West that we offer to special guests. When someone special comes over to my house for dinner there are certain things I know I have to do: cut the grass, clean up the yard, vacuum, sweep and mop and take out the trash. My daughters clean the bathrooms and straighten their rooms and my wife works her magic in the kitchen. She'll usually cook up some Arroz con Pollo, (rice and chicken) Puerto Rican style. We put away the paper plates and break out the regular plates that you actually have to wash after dinner. First century Jewish culture took all of the things we do today to another level. They went all out. There was a VIP list for those who were invited to the dinner party. Those on the list were supposed to receive special treatment. When they arrived they were greeted with a kiss and welcomed in a big way. A servant would remove their sandals and wash their feet. They would get them seated and offer them something to drink and eat.

When you know the cultural context of a passage of scripture, many times the story can become much more vivid. Luke 7:36 says, "One of the Pharisees asked Jesus to have dinner with him, so Jesus went to his home and sat down to eat." If you didn't know some of the hospitality customs and the context, you could have missed what just had happened. First of all, a lot of the Pharisees didn't like Jesus. Many people in Jesus' position would not have even accepted the invitation because of the tension that already existed. We don't know exactly why Simon the Pharisee invited Jesus over to his house but some scholars believe that some of the Pharisees were interested in His teaching or at least a bit curious. On the other hand, he may have been asking Jesus over to verbally attack Him and try to make Him look bad. We can't be sure, but what we do know is that when Jesus arrived there were no forms of customary hospitality offered to Him.

Jesus was invited, so he was on the VIP list, but Simon the host ignored Him. Nobody offered to wash His feet and no one offered Him any water to freshen up with. He was ignored as He walked in, so He went and sat down. Others saw this blatant disrespect and it immediately began to create some tension and gossip at the party. Here is another part about their culture that is very interesting and important to know. These types of dinner parties usually took place in a courtyard outside of the house and they were open to the general public. That means that anyone from the village could come to the party. But, the only people that were offered the customary hospitality and could eat the food were the people on the VIP list. But, the other people could come in and stand around the edges of the party that was in the center of the courtyard and they could watch, listen and be nosey. They didn't have wi-fi, cable or social media so the dinner parties were the place to be, even if you weren't on the VIP list.

So, you have half of the village at this dinner party and they just saw Jesus get ignored as He walks in, even though He was an invited guest. In verse 37 it starts to get real interesting. "When a certain immoral woman from that city heard He was eating there, she brought a beautiful alabaster jar filled with expensive perfume. Then she knelt behind Him at his feet, weeping. Her tears fell on His feet, and she wiped them off with her hair. Then she kept kissing His feet and putting perfume on them."

The NLT version of scripture is being nice when it says "a certain immoral woman". Other versions describe her as the town prostitute. So imagine this courtyard full of people, some VIPs and lots of regular town people and then this well known prostitute walks in the party. There were all kinds of reactions. Most people were totally upset that she was there, as she was considered immoral and dirty. Some were embarrassed because they knew her, if you know what I mean. Then you had the actual Pharisees that were religious leaders and they definitely didn't want her there, as she was an unclean outsider. But, she walks over to Jesus and she pulls out this expensive bottle of Versace perfume and starts pouring it on His feet. People gasp. This is really expensive perfume that she bought with money she earned from doing unspeakable things. How could Jesus let her do this to Him? On top of that, there was a part that most of us probably missed. She let her hair down! She was wiping Jesus' feet with it. In Middle Eastern culture letting your hair down in public was a serious no-no. Women didn't do that. That was only for the privacy of their homes. So, to recap what just happened; Jesus is on the VIP list and walks in and gets dissed. The town prostitute walks in, pulls out this expensive perfume, takes her hair bun out and whips her hair around and starts drying Jesus feet with it as she is uncontrollably weeping out loud as everyone stairs in disbelief.

Then the host of the party says, "If this man were a prophet, He would know what kind of woman is touching Him. She's a sinner!" He then says to Simon that He has something to say to him. Now, All eyes are on Jesus. What is He going to say? What is He going to do? Everyone is on the edge of their seats. They haven't seen some good drama like this in a long time. In classic Jesus form He begins to tell a story. He was about to set up Simon and drop some wisdom. He shared, "A man loaned money to two people – 500 pieces of silver to one and 50 pieces to the other. But neither of them could repay him, so he kindly forgave them both, cancelling their debts. Who do you supposed loved him more after that? Simon answered, 'I suppose the one for whom he canceled the larger debt.' 'That's right', Jesus said. Then He turned to the woman and said to Simon, 'Look at this woman kneeling here…'" Have you ever had someone talk to you, but they weren't looking at you? This is what Jesus was doing at this point. He then says, "Look at this woman…" I think there may have been some people in the crowd that still didn't get it at this point and thought that maybe Jesus was going to say something negative about the woman, but he actually does just the opposite.

Have you ever been to someone's home and they said or did some awkward things that made you feel uncomfortable? I have experienced this before, but since it was their home, I just stayed quiet and didn't say anything. I just figured I wasn't going to come back again. Well, Jesus didn't stay quiet. He actually put Simon on blast in his own home. "When I entered your home, you didn't offer me water to wash the dust from my feet, but she has washed them with her tears and wiped them with her hair. You didn't greet me with a kiss, but from the time I first came in, she has not stopped kissing my feet. You neglected the courtesy of olive oil to anoint my head, but she has anointed my feet with rare perfume." Remember all those Jewish hospitality customs I mentioned? Jesus pointed out how He was denied each of them. This would have been considered disgraceful as taking care of guests and honoring them was so important in their culture. Then Jesus tied in the story about the man that loaned two people money with the woman who showed him the hospitality. "I tell you, her sins – and they are many – have been forgiven, so she has shown me much love. But a person who is forgiven little shows only little love." Boom! Once again He is putting Simon and now the other Pharisees out there as He says the woman was forgiven many sins and she is grateful and shows much love. But, Simon and his squad think that they are all good. They don't ask for much forgiveness because they think they don't need it. As a result of their arrogance they show little love.

If it couldn't get any more intense, Jesus still had one more bomb to drop. Then He turned to the woman and said to her, "Your sins are forgiven." This set off several people at the party saying, "Who does He think He is forgiving sins?" Jesus made the town prostitute the star of this passage. She was an outsider. People had given up on her. Simon and his guests and half the village didn't want her at the dinner party. Jesus not only called Simon out and condemned him for not offering him the customary hospitality, but he lifted up this woman and applauded her actions. He esteemed a woman at a predominately male gathering. All of this was extremely counter cultural. He showed love to the loveless. Let's follow his example.

Love Lesson:

Even in the midst of tension,
Jesus showed love to those without a voice.

Love Question:

Who are the people in your community without a voice
and how could you serve them?

Love Application:

How can you apply this to your life?

Love Notes:

What stuck out to you? What else is God saying to you?

Day 17

"Our Doctor"

"Healthy people don't need a doctor – sick people do."
- Matthew 9:12 NLT

"Now He's given me vision – Now he's given me drive / Now 24/7 you'll find me on the grind / Rhyming & Writing & Preaching & Reaching the Lost / Living & Breathing & Eating & Reppin' The Cross"
- Urban D. "Hustle – Legacy Remix" (Hustle EP)

The gospel of Matthew chapter 9 tells a story of how Jesus walked up to a tax collector's booth and invited him to become His disciple. Matthew jumped up and followed Him. This would have seemed absolutely crazy to anyone alive at that time. Tax collectors were the most hated people around. They were Jews who collected taxes for the oppressive Roman Empire. These tax collectors had a set amount they had to send to Rome and the rest they could keep. They made themselves rich off of the hard work of their fellow Jews. Tax collectors were basically like the mafia of Jesus's time. If you didn't pay whatever price they set for your taxes, they could have you thrown in jail by the authority of the Roman government. It was basically legalized extortion. So, why in the world would Jesus want to invite one of those thieving traitors to be part of His team? It doesn't seem like it would be popular with the public opinion. But, Jesus never seemed to care much about what people thought. He was more concerned about what His Father thought.

So why did Matthew get up and follow Him so quickly? He already knew who Jesus was as there in Capernaum was where He performed some of His greatest miracles. But, beyond recognizing this guy with the local buzz, I believe he felt something and experienced something from Jesus that he never had before. It was His love and grace that others had not extended. Jesus looked at this hated tax collector with compassion. He saw his potential, and even though he had made mistakes, Jesus knew He could transform him and use him. Although Matthew might have been living a comfortable lifestyle, he was rejected and despised by everyone. The simple words of Jesus, "Follow me" cut straight to Matthew's heart. It was like a second chance at life. Matthew was called. Jesus' invite was giving him a new family and a new future. Without a word, Matthew's heart said, "Yes! I'm down! Let's go!"

Matthew got so excited about his new relationship with Jesus and his new lifestyle that he wanted to tell all of his friends about it. This is a regular occurrence when you have someone discover the love of Christ. They get excited and want to tell others so they can also experience it. Many of you reading this can relate with this story, as that was you. Many new Christians start out with lots of zeal to reach others around them and love their city. They also may have a lot of non-Christian friends like Matthew had. Unfortunately as time goes on many Christians lose that young zeal and eventually most of the friends they have around them are Christians. Refer back to Day 1 and our comfort problem.

So Matthew was new to this Christian thing and he was on fire. He had a plan. He was going to throw this big house party and have all the tax collectors, crooks and shady business people invited. Then he was going to get Jesus to come and talk to them and hopefully they could experience what he now had. We see this unfold in Matthew 9:10, "Later, Matthew invited Jesus and His disciples to his home as dinner guests, along with many tax collectors and other disreputable sinners." So Jesus and His squad pulled up to the party and were mixing it up with all of these characters. It doesn't mean they were getting drunk or participating in any of the sinful things that may have been happening, but they were there among the people. Jesus was into building bridges and not barriers. Imagine if more Christians followed the example of Matthew and threw a house party for their non-Christian friends and had some Christian friends in the mix to show them the love of Jesus. Verse 11 reveals that Jesus was quickly criticized by religious people as it says, "But when the Pharisees saw this, they asked His disciples. 'Why does your teacher eat with such scum?'" So Jesus was being judged just because He was around these people. As you love your city there may be some religious people that may question why you would even put yourself in a situation where you are around certain kinds of people.

I love Jesus's reply. This is my favorite part; "Healthy people don't need a doctor – sick people do. Now go and learn the meaning of this scripture: 'I want you to show mercy, not offer sacrifices.' For I have come to call not those who think they are righteous, but those who know they are sinners." Drop the mic! The first part is super easy to literally understand. Jesus is hanging out with the spiritually sick people, because they need a spiritual doctor. The second part gets a little deeper as He quotes Hosea 6:6, which is a passage calling Israel to repentance. It says, "I want you to show love, not offer sacrifices. I want you to know me more than I want burnt offerings." God doesn't want a routine sacrifice or a meaningless offering. He wants us to really get to know Him personally and when we do, we will become like Him and we will show love like Him. We'll show love to the hated. We'll show love to the unlovable. We'll be able to Love Our City through His eyes of compassion.

Again and again we see Jesus go after the outsiders. They are the neighbors that everyone has written off. I've heard it said before that if you go after the people that no one wants, you will end up with the people everyone wants. It sounds like an oxy-moron, but I've seen it play out like that so many times in my own ministry over the years. We've always reached out to the urban community that is predominately unchurched and de-churched. Many of them have lots of issues and baggage. Some of them have church hurt and trust issues. Some of them have no church etiquette. Some of them are very unstable financially, emotionally and relationally. It can be hard to love people like this, but if you look throughout the gospels, these are the exact people Jesus poured into. Even Jesus' disciples were a squad of misfits. But, they were the ones that ended up changing the world. Peter and John stood before the court system of their day in Acts 4. The members of the council were astonished by the knowledge and the way they articulated themselves. How did they become so wise and confident? The second part of Acts 4:13 says, "They recognized them as men who had been with Jesus."

If you can get your neighbors with issues to spend time with Jesus, it changes the game. They begin to transform. We've watched some of the most challenging people become incredible leaders, passionate volunteers, generous givers, strategic entrepreneurs, gifted mentors and the list goes on and on. We can rally an army of volunteers to participate in Love Our City because they directly experienced the love of Christ from us. Now they want to give back and have other neighbors experience it too.

Love Lesson:

Jesus hung out with sinners.

Love Question:
- Who could you invite over to a house party that doesn't know Jesus?

Love Application:
How can you apply this to your life?

Love Notes:
What stuck out to you? What else is God saying to you?

Day 18

"Our Diversity"

"After this I saw a vast crowd, too great to count from every nation and tribe and people and language, standing in front of the throne and before the lamb. "
- **Revelation 7:9 (a) NLT**

"I am the church, You are the church / We are the Church – since our Spiritual Rebirth / It ain't the building, It ain't the steeple / Look at the Biblical context – it's the people!"
– **Urban D. "Church" (Un.orthodox Album)**

The church in America has been in decline for several decades. There are several different statistics out there. Most are in the range that 65% - 85% of churches in America are either plateaued or declining [1]. I am not trying to be a downer, I'm actually an optimist, but I'm also a realist. Yes, there are some churches that are growing, thriving and crushing it, but we have to face the brutal fact that the average church in the West is struggling. The big question is why? There are lots of different factors and research that shows it is a combination of things: break down of the family, a more secular agenda in education and entertainment, outdated approaches of churches, different sources where people get their spirituality and the list goes on and on. Why are a few churches growing and most are plateaued or declining? There are many reasons, but I believe one of the greatest ones is that many churches have looked inward and moved into self-preservation mode. In this chapter we'll focus on a few things that we've learned at our church along with several other churches we work with. These are some critical areas that are helping us effectively reach our community, grow and become healthier.

It can be challenging for many Christ-followers and churches to fully love their city when 86.3% of churches fail to have at least 20% diversity in their membership. Churches are 10 times more segregated than the neighborhoods they are in and 20 times more segregated than the nearby public schools [2]. This is one of the major reasons the church hasn't often been invited to the table to speak on issues of racism, classism and discrimination that we see flooding the daily news headlines. Many think the church has no credibility to speak on these topics, as we are one of the most segregated institutions in our country. Yet, the Bible tells us we are called to be agents of reconciliation.

The church has a crisis with the younger generations not attending and leaving at alarming rates. 59% of millennials raised in church have dropped out [3]. Research shows that many of them are uncomfortable with the lack of diversity. Dave Travis, the CEO of Leadership Network said, "Younger generations have come of age with diversity as an expected condition. If they look around and see a homogeneous congregation they tend to discount the effectiveness of the church experience." Younger generations live in diversity and when many of them step in a church and everyone looks the same it feels really weird. The church I lead is made up of people mostly under 40 years old. One consistent comment that people make is how they love the diversity at our church. Our church reflects our city. We must intentionally make changes so our churches can look more like the communities around them. It must go farther then just putting a few token people on the platform. There must be diversity at the leadership table helping make decisions. These different perspectives are critical to help churches navigate language, responses and even illustrations in the polarized world that we currently live in.

We shouldn't strive to become more diverse because it is now trending. This was Jesus' heart long before it became culturally popular. This was always His plan as he told the disciples to go and make disciples of all nations. The New Testament churches were reflective of their communities. Of the nine churches in the book of Acts, seven were multi-ethnic. The other two were not because they were in mono-ethnic communities.

When we think about the New Testament church, we can quickly think about the church in Jerusalem that started in Acts chapter 2 on the day of Pentecost. That first day alone it grew to 3,000 people. Many of those people spoke different languages and were from different countries as they were in the city to celebrate the festivals. The first day of the first New Testament church was multi-ethnic and multi-lingual. There are several other passages in the book of Acts that talk about thousands more being added to the church in Jerusalem on several occasions. But, they weren't the most influential church in the New Testament.

The church in Antioch sent out the most missionaries and made the largest impact. They were the church that commissioned and sent out Paul and others to spread the gospel on missionary journeys. Their church was multi-ethnic, multi-generational and multi-class. It all started with their leadership team. It always must start from the top down. Maybe you have never noticed the beginning of Acts chapter 13. "Among the prophets and teachers of the church at Antioch of Syria were Barnabas, Simeon (called "the black man"), Lucius (from Cyrene) Manaen (the child-hood companion of King Herod Antipas), and Saul." Barnabas was a Levite from Cyprus, which is an island in the Mediterranean. Simeon has a Jewish name, but he was called Niger, which literally meant black, because of his darker complexion. He was most likely of African descent. Lucius was from Cyrene, which is the capital of Libya in North Africa. Manaen was a Jew raised with Herod the Great. The pastoral leadership team of the church of Antioch was multi-ethnic. You had European/Mediterranean (Barnabas), African (Simeon, Lucius) and Middle Eastern (Manaen, Saul). The leadership of the church of Antioch reflected the ethnic and cultural diversity of the city of Antioch.

When the leadership team is diverse, their missions' strategy is usually more diverse. They care about reaching people that are from their background and there is a greater awareness of various people groups right in their own community and abroad that need to hear about the love of Christ. The church I lead is far from perfect, but we excel in diversity. Our staff, leadership, and volunteer teams are all diverse across the board. In our early days, much of this was organic as many of us grew up in the hip-hop generations, so diversity happened more naturally. Our church has always had some hip-hop flavor in our worship services, so that automatically attracted a diverse crowd. As we grew in size and in our theology we became more intentional. Our studies led us to see an even stronger case for church diversity in the scripture. This is one of our church's 7 core values. We regularly celebrate it and teach and preach about it. Becoming and/or balancing a diverse church is not always easy as there are many different views, traditions, preferences, and politics in the congregation. If you'd like to learn more about this, I highly recommend Mark Deymaz's book "Building a healthy Multi-Ethnic Church".

Love Lesson:

New Testament churches were reflective of their communities.

Love Question:

What are some reasons that churches
in your community may be struggling?

Love Application:

How can you apply this to your life?

Love Notes:

What stuck out to you? What else is God saying to you?

Day 19
"Our Why"

"Instead, you must worship Christ as Lord of your life.
And if someone asks about your hope as a believer,
always be ready to explain it."
- 1 Peter 3:15 NLT

"We live in the most advanced culture this planet has ever seen / But
it's unheard / That's absurd / Man how could it be? / It's the powers
that be / Broadband and 4G / That reach right into your home, your
pocket, your screen"
- Urban D. "Un.heard" (Un.heard album)

As we Love Our City it is important that we know the why. It is important that leaders equip their churches to understand the theology behind it. We can't assume everyone gets it. It is important that believers seek out resources and tools to sharpen their faith. The word "love" and the concept of loving other people is very fluid in our pluralistic culture. If we aren't careful, our outreach efforts can turn into a social justice effort that is void of the gospel. We closely monitor our "seed planting" approach with Love Our City, as we don't want it to slip into a community service project with no spiritual purpose. Addressing this is regularly on the menu at our church. We are also intentional to do a series leading up to Love Our City week so we can biblically break down why we are doing it. We have done several "Love Our City series" at our church. The latest one is available for you to watch on our youtube channel (crossover813). Plus, we released the outlines, transcripts, artwork, and small group videos and curriculum so other churches can use it and tweak it for their context. You may currently be going through the series at your church as we have a lot of churches joining us in the Love Our City movement.

People are receiving more information than we ever have in the history of civilization. The growth in the internet, TV channels and smart phones means that we now receive five times as much information as we did in 1986 [1]. But, that pales in comparison to the growth in the amount of information we produce through our email, text and social media platforms. Everyday the average person produces six newspapers worth of information compared with just two and a half pages just 24 years ago. That's nearly a 200-fold increase [2]. People need filters more than ever for all the information being consumed and produced. We need the why. We need solid teaching and theology to help us stay on track in a world full of counterfeit gospels.

I'm a strong advocate for apologetics (learning to defend your faith). Growing up in the church has made me realize that the church overall has done a poor job of equipping people to be able to articulate why they believe what they believe. We live in an age that everyone questions everything. I don't think that is necessarily bad, but the danger is that people can now look in so many different places for answers. Many people ask Google before they ask God. We must prepare ourselves, and believers in our churches with the right answers and the right information. **1 Peter 3:15** tells us,

"Instead, you must worship Christ as Lord of your life. And if someone asks about your hope as a believer, always be ready to explain it."

Our church is intentional to offer apologetics classes, resources and even a Sunday message series into our annual calendar. We have used resources from Ravi Zacharias, Josh McDowell and many others. Many of our series present how we got the Bible, how we know it hasn't been changed, and that we can trust it. We share evidence through history and archeology. We share how we can reason and find proof that brings us to an intellectual decision that the resurrection of Jesus really took place. We have also done several series that simply answered questions. In the summer of 2018 we did a series entitled "You asked for it". People emailed their questions about God, the Bible and how that connects to our everyday lives. It was powerful as we were able to bring up "touchy" issues, because they asked for it! They wanted to know what God's word really said about it. Of course when you talk about hot-topic issues you must always approach it with love, grace and humility.

In the fall of 2017, I had the opportunity to travel with a group of Christian leaders and apologists to Israel. It was my first time to visit and it was absolutely amazing. I could write a book on just that. It was such a powerful experience that brought the Bible to life in new ways. I also learned so much about the Israeli and Palestinian conflict from people on both sides of it. What made it especially incredible was being on a trip with world-renowned apologetic authors and speakers whose material I regularly read and used. These guys were geniuses. The conversations were rich and enlightening. One of the guys on the trip, Sean McDowell, dropped a practical gem that sums up today's chapter, "No single apologetics or evangelism method works for everyone. People are different." As a believer we must constantly strengthen our faith, add new tools and sharpen the old ones. We must engage different people with different methods as we share with them "our why".

> *"Love is a command, not just a feeling. Somehow, in the romantic world of music and theater we have made love to be what it is not. We have mixed it with beauty and charm and sensuality and contact that we have robbed it of its higher call of cherishing and nurturing."* **- Ravi Zacharias**

Love Lesson:

We need solid teaching and apologetics to equip us in a world full of counterfeit gospels.

Love Question:

When people ask you tough questions about God and the Bible are you equipped to properly answer them?

Love Application:

How can you apply this to your life?

Love Notes:

What stuck out to you? What else is God saying to you?

Day 20

"Our Response"

"Understand this, my dear brothers and sisters:
You must be quick to listen, slow to speak and slow to get angry."
- James 1:19 NLT

"What if gardens replaced empty lots / No more drugs, no more
violence, no more crooked cops / Just mentors, classes and job
training / Not a hand out, but a hand up to a life that's sustaining"
- Urban D. "New Life, New Fam, New City (ReBuild Album)

What do we say when an unarmed Black man gets shot by White police officers? What do we say when two Black men get arrested for sitting in a Starbucks? What do we say after the Charlottesville protest left dozens injured and someone lost their life? What do we say after dozens of students get killed in a school shooting? These are critical moments that the church can and should speak into. Our church has not talked about it every single time that something has happened, because it seems there is something happening almost weekly. We never want that to overshadow the gospel, but we want to speak the gospel into those situations as often as possible. We can't ignore it as so many Christians and churches do, but what we say and how we say it are super important. That's why I stress that having different ethnic groups at the leadership table is so critical. Our multi-ethnic, multi-generational, multi-class church has responded in a variety of ways over the past several years and we've all learned some new things in our leadership meetings that have helped us address it even better. We've changed our direction a number of times due to new information and new perspectives that were presented as we planned, prepared, and prayed.

We must learn to listen. Most of us can grow in this area. When we hear about something or see something we don't always respond like James 1:19 instructs us. We must remember that we haven't experienced what everyone else has. Although I may have experienced some discrimination in my life, it is nothing like what a 75 year-old African American man in my church has been through. We all have lenses that determine how we look at things. They are shaped by our life experiences. When we start a relationship with Christ we become part of His family, but that does not change the color of our skin or the experiences we went through. We must learn to listen to others with different experiences, ideas, and even political leanings. When we truly put ourselves in their shoes and empathize with them it can be a game changer.

In the summer of 2016 there were several incidents of police shooting unarmed black men, along with police being shot, widespread protests and social media videos going viral. There was a lot of tension and fear in many communities. I wanted to call a town hall meeting with police officers, city leaders and the community to talk about it in our city before something popped off. I first had a meeting with some of our leadership team. Several of us felt it could be great for our church people and at the same time be a powerful outreach to the community. One of the guys in that meeting is a leader of the NAACP in our city. He liked the idea, but warned us about some past issues that happened in our community that most likely would draw out a few disgruntled people that would seek to highjack the meeting. He saw this happen at multiple events he had been a part of around the city. We were totally unaware of this possibility, but when he laid out the facts, we knew we had to tweak the plan and use wisdom. We decided for it to be an in house family meeting and instead of us doing it on a different day, we interrupted a message series and did it on Sunday morning in all three of our services.

We had a panel with a city of Tampa Police officer, a Hillsborough County Sheriff officer, our city council woman, our congressmen and our business district leader. Myself, and my executive pastor were bookends on the panel asking questions on behalf of our community and people. We did no promotion, besides a short Facebook live post that morning. Channel 10 News immediately called us asking if they could come. Who knew the local news was following our Facebook page? I think churches many times underestimate their influence. We agreed to let the news come with the stipulation that they could only interview people we chose. We were not going to let them walk around our lobby and ask questions to random people. The panel went incredible and the unexpected news story also came out great. When you have the right people around your leadership table and you are guided by God's spirit, some real God moments can occur.

There are a variety of other ways our church has addressed current issues in culture. Sometimes it was simply acknowledging what happened and praying for justice and peace. Other times it was weaved into a sermon. Sometimes it was an entire message. Shortly after the Charlottesville incident we did a series entitled "Fake News" and we played off of that popular term and talked about fake news that is said about the Bible and Christianity. One of the week's titles was – "Fake News: The Bible supports slavery and White supremacy". We went into detail about the context of slavery in the scripture and talked about the differences between Old Testament slavery, colonial slavery and modern day sex slavery. We also addressed the bad theology that was formerly taught about the curse of Noah's son Ham. In the past, some churches, seminaries, and even Study Bibles taught that because of what happened in this passage, all dark skinned people were cursed and would be servants. Unfortunately, this passage was wrongly used to justify slavery in the past. Black people, White people, and people of every shade were happy to see their church addressing it and explaining it in a balanced way.

These are issues that every church may not want to talk about, but we need to. There are more and more attacks from culture against the Bible and the church. They seek to discredit Christianity. With all the false narratives out there, it's so important that we educate our people with the truth so we can have a proper response.

> *"In many dialogues on race, we don't realize that we don't speak the same language. We have to define our terms to start to understand one another and more so the visible and invisible systems we all live in."* **- Eric Mason**

Love Lesson:

We must respond with discernment and learn to listen to the Holy Spirit as we learn to listen to other people's perspectives.

Love Question:

Have you had an experience that you may have responded incorrectly in the past? What did you learn?

Love Application:

How can you apply this to your life?

Love Notes:

What stuck out to you? What else is God saying to you?

Day 21
"Our Taste"

"Taste and see that the Lord is good.
Oh, the joys of those who take refuge in him!"
- Psalm 34:8 NLT

"Like some Pollo (Chicken) straight off the grill / La palabra de Dios
(The word of God) always gives you a balanced meal /
That's seasoned with love like Adobo / That why we take
this message global / Actions speak louder than vocals
I pray you see our actions clearer than bi-focals"
- Urban D. "Love Revolution" (Un.heard Album)

You have flavor! That's right! Each of you reading this has a unique spice to you. God created you that way. You have some special gifts and talents that he has blessed you with so you could use them to give others a taste of God's love. Jesus told us in Matthew 5:13 that we are the salt of the earth. He meant that His disciples' good deeds would have a huge positive impact in the world around them for the glory of God. Now with this declaration there was also a warning. Jesus told us to be careful that we don't lose our flavor. He makes the point that without our flavor we can become useless like the lukewarm water we talked about in Day 1. Some of you may have lost some of your flavor, but I believe that God is going to use Love Our City to revive some of your gifts, talents, and calling.

Crossover Church has been taught to Love Our City through our everyday lifestyles. In addition there are weekly programs and regular outreach events for our church family to plug into and show love. One of the biggest impacts has been the "Love Our City week", where the majority of the church volunteers to complete community service projects in the district around the church. We are also joined by hundreds of business partners, ministries and residents that volunteer with us. We are in a very diverse area so our strategy is to reach as many different people groups as possible. Our leadership team put up a white board and made categories of different tribes in our neighborhood. As we came up with project ideas we put them in those categories. The demographics in our district include college students, business people, single mothers, first responders, teachers, families in poverty, immigrants, retired people, tourists and homeless. Some of these people live in our community, some of them work here and some of them play here. We wanted to intentionally find ways to give them a taste of the love of Christ through tangible acts of kindness.

Hosting a Love Our City week or a one-day outreach is a great way to also give people a taste of serving. Most people are already busy and overwhelmed in their daily lives. When they hear about opportunities to get involved in a consistent serving position at a church or a non-profit, many can quickly write it off as they feel they just don't have time. Of course, we will always find time for the things we think are truly important. Creating a one time opportunity for people to serve can be much more attractive and can open the door for people to put their toe in the water. We've found that if they have a good experience when they serve, it is something that quickly moves up on their priority list. There have been several people that were not consistently serving that started doing it regularly after Love Our City week. We had one lady take off a few days of work to serve that week and she loved it so much that she is now a major part of the Love Our City planning team.

If you are reading this and you are not regularly serving at your local church in some capacity, I pray this book will nudge you to move into the right fit that God has for you. It can be tempting to think that your church doesn't need you, or God can't use you, but don't fall for that lie. You are not reading this book by accident. If you got all the way to Day 21, God wants to use you to love your city in unique ways that he created you to. I encourage you and challenge you to get off the bench and jump into the game!

Love Lesson:

You have some special gifts and talents that God has blessed you with so you could use them to give others a taste of his love.

Love Question:

How are you regularly giving people a taste of God's love?

Love Application:

How can you apply this to your life?

Love Notes:

What stuck out to you? What else is God saying to you?

Watch the video at www.youtube.com/urband813

Our neighbors have all kinds of _____, but yet all kinds of _____. As our character becomes more like Christ – our vision _____ and we can begin to see people and situations the way that Jesus sees them.

Read the Gospel of John Chapter 8

Example after example we see Jesus offering radical
___Grace_____; from the woman at the well with 5 husbands, to Matthew the hated tax collector, to the town prostitute at Simon's dinner party.

The WHY is super important. Sometimes we forget to answer the WHY and we just want to jump into the ___how_____.

"And if someone asks about your hope as a believer, always be ready to explain it. But do this in a gentle and respectful way." - 1 Peter 3:15-15 NLT

We should never look to start a fight or win a debate, but to respectfully engage with people and explain the ___why_____.

"I am the way, the truth and the life. No one can come to the Father except through me." - John 14:6 NLT

Discussion Questions

1. In what ways has God changed your vision in how you see people and situations?

Read the Gospel of John 8:1-11

2. Has someone ever shown you grace (given you something you didn't deserve?) What happened?

Read 1 Peter 3:15-16

3. Have you ever had someone ask you a spiritual question and you didn't know the answer, or you struggled to explain it?

4. Has someone asked you a spiritual question and you were able to explain it well?

5. What are some of the fake gospels or false religions that may be popular in your city?

6. Are you confident enough in your faith to have a conversation with someone from a different religion?

Day 22

"Our Atmosphere"

"Even though I am a free man with no master,
I have become a slave to all people to bring many to Christ."
- 1 Corinthians 9:19 NLT

"If the culture can rep cribs, cars and ice / Hip-Hop's about
expression – you spit your life / Express the pain, the stress, the strife /
Then I can only be real and celebrate the Christ!"
- Urban D. "Celebrate the Culture" (The Crossover Cypha Vol. 5)

We have the ability and the responsibility to change the atmosphere. If you are a Christ-follower you have the Holy Spirit living in you. He can empower you in every situation you enter. Many of us regularly enter drama filled environments at work, school, or home. We can change the atmosphere. It may not be easy. It may be met with resistance. It may take time. But, God can use us to bring a shift and set a new tone. I've watched this happen time and time again, as a Christ-follower would start working in a new position, start attending a new school, or start playing on a new team. I've watched it happen with a new believer that would begin to change the atmosphere in their home, as their walk with Christ grew stronger.

We have to learn to read the atmosphere as we step into it so we can better serve. This was Paul's strategy as he shared in 1 Corinthians chapter 9:19-22, "Even though I am a free man with no master, I have become a slave to all people to bring many to Christ. When I was with the Jews, I lived like a Jew to bring the Jews to Christ. When I was with those who follow the Jewish law, I too lived under that law. Even though I am not subject to the law, I did this so I could bring to Christ those who are under the law. When I am with the Gentiles who do not follow the Jewish law, I too live apart from that law so I can bring them to Christ. But I do not ignore the law of God; I obey the law of Christ. When I am with those who are weak, I share their weakness, for I want to bring the weak to Christ. Yes, I try to find common ground with everyone, doing everything I can to save some."

As you step into different spaces, there will be different ways to talk and respond to become an atmosphere changer. I've had to learn this over the years as I started as a youth pastor and a Hip-Hop artist. I was predominately working with teenagers. Eventually I got pushed into being the lead pastor at my church. I had to learn to become a better communicator with adults. It was different, but I learned how to still be myself. There are times when I'm in the hood with neighborhood residents, while there are times I'm in the board room with business leaders. Sometimes I'm wearing jeans and a T-shirt, while other times I'm throwing on a blazer on top of that T-Shirt to dress it up. I'm still being myself, but I've learned how to change language so I can communicate with different people groups and change the atmosphere in our diverse city.

Paul also learned to read the atmosphere when he first went to Athens. When he first got there he was deeply disturbed by the spiritual environment. There were idols everywhere in the city and people were far from God. The scripture tells us that he took some time and studied the people, spoke to people and tried to read the temperature of the culture. Once he got his bearings he started to turn up the heat. He gathered a large crowd where everybody went to politic and debate. Acts 17:22-23 in the Message version says, "So Paul took his stand in the open space at the Areopagus and laid it out for them. 'It is plain to see that you Athenians take your religion seriously. When I arrived here the other day, I was fascinated with all the shrines I came across. And then I found one inscribed, to the god nobody knows. I'm here to introduce you to this God so you can worship intelligently, know who you're dealing with.'" Paul drew them in with something familiar from their culture. A little farther down in the passage he even quoted one of their poets. If Paul was here today he might be quoting a chart topping rapper. At the end of his presentation there were some that laughed, some that said they wanted to hear more, and some that became believers that day. Paul didn't just take the temperature, he became the thermostat and turned up the heat and several people became part of the church in that city.

In 2010, our church retrofitted a 43,000 square foot former Toys R' Us store in the heart of Tampa's urban community. Many of the stores fled to the new malls that were built in the suburbs. The neighborhood's nickname was Suitcase City due to its transient nature. The poverty rate in the immediate neighborhood was over 60%. It wasn't a good neighborhood to move a church to but we knew we were called there to change the environment and set a new atmosphere. At first, it seemed overwhelming as there were so many needs and the problems were so layered and complex. But we just kept seeking God's plan, loving people, meeting needs and making disciples. It takes time, but eight years later we see a definite shift in our community. There is a lot of work to do, but the change is happening.

Love Our City is an atmosphere changing event in our community. We unleash over 1,000 volunteers into our neighborhood. As they are serving people all week long it shifts the tone. Get ready as doing Love Our City will change the atmosphere in your hood. God will work in your people, through your people and on the people they touch.

Love Lesson:

We have to learn to read the atmosphere
as we step into it so we can better serve.

Love Question:

What is the temperature for God in your neighborhood, work place, school and church? How can we become more of a thermostat and turn up the heat?

Love Application:

How can you apply this to your life?

Love Notes:

What stuck out to you? What else is God saying to you?

Day 23

"Our Reputation"

*"Your love for one another will prove to the world
that you are my disciples."*
- John 13:35 NLT

*"Come to Crossover every Wednesday night (3xs) /
All day everyday we represent Christ."*
- Urban D. "Open Mic Chant" (Regularly used live at service)

There are many people that pass by your church each day and have no idea what actually goes on inside. They have never been inside and a lot of them don't plan to ever come. Why is this? We live in a culture where church is becoming more and more irrelevant. A recent pew study found that millennials are leaving the church in droves. It also found declining church attendance in every age group. [1]. So if people are leaving and not interested in coming back, then let's go to them. That's what Love Our City is all about! That's what we are supposed to be doing anyways, but refer to Day 1...we've gotten comfortable. When we get out of the seats and into the streets we can change people's perception of Christians and the church. They can experience the love of Christ and this can be a catalyst to change their life forever. This will not only enhance your church's reputation, but the church as a whole.

Our church has grown in size, influence and impact because of our reputation of loving our city. When something good is happening, people will talk about it. When people want to do something in your community, they usually will want to talk with the community anchors. We have watched this happen as our reputation grew. Our church has been approached to partner with multiple major organizations in our community including the city of Tampa. Why did this happen? They kept saying, "I'm hearing about all the great things you are doing for our community. Thank you! We want to work with you."

Our city was impacted by hurricane Irma in September of 2017. We are grateful that the damage was not as bad as was originally predicted, but there were many people without power for up to a week. Our church assessed the needs along with the city and business leaders and we determined the biggest need was providing hot meals, groceries, water and a place to come and cool off. Fortunately, our church was in one of the few places that had power. We sprung into action to Love Our City and provide hurricane relief from our location. The local business alliance and city partnered with us and helped spread the word. Our site became the official hurricane relief effort of North Tampa. We served hundreds of families and all of it was paid for through the donations of local businesses.

I recently went to a small private dinner with the CEO of Busch Gardens and a few other CEOs and business leaders. There were only about a dozen of us. My executive pastor and I were the only ones there from a church. They wanted us in the room because they like what we're doing and they want to partner more in the future. We've had government agencies support our Back 2 School Jam, and we've had secular corporations write us significant checks. We've been invited to sit on boards making major decisions that are reshaping our community. We regularly are asked to open our city council meetings in prayer. These doors have opened because of our approach. We are here to love and serve our city. When you consistently are doing that, people will notice. There are some strategic things you can do that I talk about in the leaders guide, but a lot of this will organically begin to happen.

At the end of Love Our City week we throw a big party. When is that party? It's at our Sunday services. We didn't create a separate event, we wanted them to come and experience our unique Sunday services and see what we were really all about. We have incredible worship and arts, a highlight video from the week, a creative message, free food, bounce houses, photo booths and more. Some of our parties have even included our mayor, city councilmen and several leaders from the community. We see hundreds of people that we touched come out to our services. It's a big celebration where we clearly share the gospel and talk about the love of Christ. Our rhythm is doing Love Our City week leading up to Easter Sunday. We've found that gives us even more momentum, as it is already the biggest Sunday of the year for us. We've also found people in our city are more receptive to come and visit on Easter. In addition, it engages our people to get them inviting others at their jobs, schools and neighborhoods as we have so much excitement going into our Easter services. This past Easter we had our largest attendance in our history and over 100 people indicated they started a relationship with Christ by filling out a card and receiving a free copy of my book "Next Steps on Your Spiritual Journey". We followed up with all of those people and the Sunday after Easter we had 88 people get baptized.

There are no strings attached with Love Our City, as people don't have to do anything now or ever to receive the blessing we are giving them. But we are intentional in inviting them to the party. Every time we do an outreach event, we are always putting something in their hand inviting them to what is next. It's totally up to them if they come. We are only planting a seed and praying that God will move in their hearts. Our strategy is to build a relationship with them and continue to cultivate that so they can get to know us, and the God we love and serve.

Love Lesson:

When we get out of the seats and into the streets we can change people's perception of Christians and the church.

Love Question:

What is the reputation of Christians and churches in your city? How do you think a Love Our City week could impact it?

Love Application:

How can you apply this to your life?

Love Notes:

What stuck out to you? What else is God saying to you?

Hip-Hop Artist Dee-1

Day 24

"Our Prayer"

"After sending them (the crowd) home, he (Jesus) went up into the hills by himself to pray. Night fell while he was there alone."
- **Matthew 14:23 NLT**

"I never start moving until I pray / Sparking evidently at the top of the day / I'm gathering wisdom for the words to say / Show the way / Map the play / Okay!"
- **Urban D. "Hustle" (Un.orthodox album)**

Before, during, and after we Love Our City we should always pray. This was a model that Jesus set for us. During his three and a half years of ministry he was incredibly busy, but there were several times recorded in the gospels where he broke away from the crowd to get alone and pray. There were times when it was early in the morning before his ministry launched for the day and other times when it was late at night after a long day of ministry. We can see several key moments throughout Jesus' life that he prayed: at his baptism, when he was choosing the disciples, when others were in need, at the last supper, in the garden of Gethsemane and on the cross. The gospels are full of lessons on prayer. Jesus taught us to pray without a desire to be seen (Matt. 6:5-6). He told us to reconcile with others before praying (Matt. 5:23-24). Jesus showed us to pray before important decisions (Luke 6:12-13). He taught us not to pray with empty phrases (Matt. 6:7). Jesus also challenged us to be bold and believe that God will answer our prayers (Mark 11:24).

As you are gearing up to love your city you need to get spiritually ready. We could have everything organized with community service projects, volunteers and resources we are giving away. But, if we do it in our own strength and strategies it will not have the impact it was meant to. We must intentionally get prayed up. It's important that we do this personally and corporately. Our church has put on lots of large events over the years from outreaches to conferences. We usually will have hundreds of volunteers involved and there are lots of moving parts. There has been some times that in our busyness we forgot to cover the event in prayer like we should have. In those events we noticed it either didn't have the same spiritual impact or there was a bad vibe with some negativity or disorganization.

All of us have busy seasons in our lives. Those are the times we need to make sure that we spend consistent time communicating with our Creator. When our schedules are more packed than normal it can put us in a vulnerable place as we are out of our normal rhythm. Sometimes those seasons can be draining and other times those seasons can be exciting and full of momentum. When you are working on something you are passionate about it can be a lot of fun. I have to admit as a leader I love momentum. But, momentum can be dangerous. It can make us think we are better than we are. It can hide our issues. It can even cause us to get prideful. The thing that will keep us grounded in busy seasons is prayer. No matter how busy we are, we have to carve out time to spend with Jesus. That must become a non-negotiable in our lives.

In the beginning of 2018 I attended a business leaders event that helped us set goals for the New Year. Each speaker that got up shared about their personal prayer and devotional time that they did each morning. I am an artist, so I'm more of a night person, so getting up earlier to pray didn't exactly fit my preference of later in the day. But, God spoke to me that morning and challenged me to step into a more intimate prayer life in this new season. I knew it would stretch me, but I was hungry to get more intimate with God. Every morning I get up and head over to my prayer closet and pull out my journal and I write down a blessing for the day at the top. I'm currently up to blessing #191. Then I pray, I listen, I read and I journal. I'm reading the Bible again from the beginning this year. It has breathed new life into my relationship with Jesus that has now been over two decades. God will show himself to you in deeper ways when you press in. If you don't already have a regular prayer and devotional rhythm, then you need to create one, and if you do have one, God may switch it up and reorganize it like he did for me.

As you and your church or small group get ready to love your city I encourage you to personally get prayed up and also spend some time together praying. Our church does a prayer night in the weeks leading up to the week. Then when it is happening, we pray for every single group that goes out and does a community service project. Our leaders send them out with a blessing as everyone first meets in our church lobby to get their t-shirts, supplies, leaders and teammates. I'm praying for every person who reads this book, every church that does Love Our City and every person who gets touched by it. Let's go!

Love Lesson:

Jesus regularly broke away from the crowd to get alone to spend time in prayer.

Love Question:

What does your regular prayer rhythm look like? How could you take it deeper?

Love Application:

How can you apply this to your life?

Love Notes:

What stuck out to you? What else is God saying to you?

Day 25

"Our Hand Up"

*"Don't look out only for your own interests,
but take an interest in others, too."*
- Philippians 2:4 NLT

*"Our culture is opposite of Philippians 2:3 / Where Paul says –
think about you, before I think about me / Check Nehemiah 5 –
he confronted injustice / Stood up for the forgotten,
we need to discuss this…"*
- Urban D. "Empowering Others" (ReBuild Album)

We hand out a lot of things during Love Our City week. It is an initial touch to our community. In many cases it is meeting critical needs for people. But we don't want to stop at just a hand out. We want to also give a hand up. Because they will need groceries next month, they will need more Christmas presents next December. They will need a backpack next school year and they might get really upset if all the purple ones are gone. We have to be careful that we are not feeding a poverty mindset. If you only create constant systems where you are just giving things out, you can enable people to continue to stay in the same place. It can build entitlement and apathy.

You can't meet every type of need in the city. It's impossible. That's why it is so important to build partnerships with other organizations and ministries in your community that are meeting needs. You don't need to duplicate services. In most communities there are already some great programs to help give a hand up. Find ways to support those organizations by serving them, funding them and sending people their way. Of course, you need to vet them and make sure they are safe, excellent and not leading people down a different spiritual path. We don't have GED classes at our church, because there are several good ones in our neighborhood to which we refer people. We partner with several of our local Community Development Corporations to host job training classes and empowerment classes in our facility and at their locations. Research who is doing good work in your community and see how you can help each other. Research what the needs are in your community and where the gaps are. God may be calling you to start something new that fills a void.

When loving your city gets in the DNA of your church, you'll begin to see God give visions to individuals and families to meet deeper needs in your community. We have created an environment for this, as I'm a kingdom entrepreneur. My mind is always turning to create new ways to help other leaders win, to reach more people and to creatively develop new streams of funding to help us accomplish the vision. They say you attract other people like you. My church has a growing base of entrepreneurs in both business and artistry. But, I'm especially excited, as there has been a new group of entrepreneurs rising up the past few years. They are starting their own non-profit organizations to meet needs in our city they are passionate about.

I remember when the Morgans first started attending our church over a dozen years ago shortly after I became the lead pastor. Brainard Morgan worked in the air conditioning industry and shared this dream about wanting to start his own A/C Company. He started doing some side jobs and soon built it up to step out on faith and become a small business owner. It was humble beginnings as his office was in a shed in his back yard. He has learned a lot about business in the past decade. Fast forward to now and he has dozens of employees. As their business has grown over the years their generosity has grown. When many people move into new economic brackets they continually move into bigger houses and nicer cars. There is nothing wrong with upgrading, but when God increases your resources, you should become an even bigger conduit to be a blessing to others. The scripture teaches us that where much is given, much is required. It's been exciting to watch this couple dream about the difference they could make in our community. Brainard's wife Nan has a passion to help women coming out of the sex industry. She has been dreaming of starting a transitional home that will help them integrate back into society after they get out of a program. This dream became a reality as they purchased a house three blocks from our church building. They completely remodeled it and they started a non-profit called "Chosen Treasures." It partners with our church's women's ministry "Chosen" to disciple these ladies in their walk with Christ.

Damon had been in prison for 17 years. He was incarcerated for selling large amounts of drugs. He was a street-smart guy with a strong business sense, but he was involved in illegal businesses. When he got to prison he was still arrogant and far from God, but eventually he was humbled and submitted his life to Christ. Damon started helping inmates start legit businesses while in prison. If anyone had an idea, they went to Damon as he was the man that could help them put it together. When he was released a few years ago he started his own non-profit "Inc to Inc" (Incarcerated to Incorporated). Damon helps people getting out of prison. They sit with him and share their passion and skills and he puts together a business plan and helps them set up their companies with all the proper paperwork. It is an amazing program that helps former inmates find their life purpose and permanently stay out of the prison system.

There are several others starting non-profits to help juveniles aging out of the foster system, juveniles getting out of the detention center, orphans in Haiti and even a girl that is repurposing wedding flowers to give to single moms in the community. So many creative ideas are forming to meet needs right in our neighborhood. Our church supports them, prays for them, encourages them and rallies around them in many ways. Some of these up and coming non-profits get resources and office space from a local partner "The Underground" that is a hub for faith-based non-profits in our community. We can't meet every need but with creative collaboration we can watch God gracefully weave some beautiful things together to give a real hand up in our cities.

"Betterment does for others. Development maintains the long view and looks to enable others to do for themselves. Betterment improves conditions. Development strengthens capacity. Betterment gives a man a fish. Development teaches a man how to fish." **- Bob Lupton**

Love Lesson:

You can't just stop at a hand out. You must meet deeper needs and give a hand up to help people become self-sustainable.

Love Question:

What are some ways you, your family, your small group or your church could help give people a "hand up" in your city?

Love Application:

How can you apply this to your life?

Love Notes:

What stuck out to you? What else is God saying to you?

Pastor Tommy & Tampa Mayor Bob Buckhorn at Crossover

Day 26

"Our Partnerships & Projects"

"Two can accomplish more than twice as much as one, for the results can be much better."
- Ecclesiastes 4:9 TLB

"We go together like chicken and teriyaki / Greeks and Soulvaki / Canadians and ice hockey / like helmets and Kawasaki / like vinyl and disc jockey / We go together like / Philadelphia and Rocky"
- Urban D. "We Go Together Like" (The Tranzlation album)

I f you've read this far in the book I know you are excited and ready to make an impact. You may have a lot of questions about the details and how to do Love Our City in your community. It seems like a lot of work, and it is, but if you have systems in place it can run smoothly no matter how large it grows. When you work together as a team you can accomplish much more like the scripture says, "Two can accomplish more than twice as much as one, for the results can be much better." We are not meant to do life and do ministry alone. Each of us has unique gifts, talents and strengths. When we partner, there is so much more than we can accomplish as a team. You will be amazed with how much you can get done with a focused group of people.

What can Love Our City projects look like? Here are a few examples of some of our most popular ones: knock knock groceries are where we deliver free groceries unexpectedly to over one thousand homes and apartments. We love to see the surprised look on people's faces when we show up with a bag of groceries for them. Pay it forward projects are all over the neighborhood at coffee shops, gas stations, Laundromats, movie theaters, restaurants, bus terminals and grocery stores. In each of those places we're paying for their coffee, gas, washing machines, movie tickets, bus passes, etc. We've found that an appreciation gift bag to go along with it is a huge hit. Inside of those gift bags we include bottled water, a candy bar, an invite to the Love Our City party (our Sunday services) and possibly even a gift card. We also do appreciation lunches for teachers, fire fighters, police officers and employees throughout our district. We feed the homeless and we feed college students. We give out bottled water and free prayer. Some of the ladies from our women's ministry even go into local strip clubs and give gift bags to the workers and offer prayer. Well over 10k people from all different walks of life are impacted during those seven days in our neighborhood.

Our church paid the cost of Love Our City week the first year. We casted the vision and did a special offering campaign and everything was fully paid for due to the generosity of our church. As the reputation grew the second year, the church only paid for a little over

50%. That number continues to drop as we have corporate sponsors and donors that are coming along side us to be a part of it. Local small businesses as well as non-profits and big companies partnered with us. Several of them donated money or items and brought a team of volunteers to serve with us. The reputation and excitement are growing with people inside and outside of our church. People want to be a part of it.

We have created a separate leaders kit that gives all the details and logistics on how we execute Love Our City. It shares how we vision cast, raise money and develop corporate and community partnerships. It also shares the nuts and bolts on how to set up the projects, contact the sites, get people signed up, train leaders and volunteers. We include our budget and how we added close to 40 new projects one year and spent $4,000 less than the previous year! We share everything we've learned and are currently learning so you don't have to make the mistakes we did. We'll show you how to maximize every dollar to make the biggest impact and to how we got close to 80% of our church involved. Our desire is for Love Our City to become a movement that will help churches reach people for Christ and truly change their communities and change the reputation of the church. We want to see you win! The leaders kit is available at the www.loveourcitybook.com website.

Love Our City week accomplishes so many things. First and foremost it brings glory to God. It brings a message of hope to the city; it meets tangible needs for so many; it empowers volunteers, brings people together and it gives the church an incredible reputation. There is a trickle down effect that steadily happens throughout the year with people connecting at the church because they or someone they know was touched at Love Our City. I encourage you to pray about joining us to do Love Our City in your community with your church, small group or ministry.

Love Lesson:

When we come together there is so much more than we can accomplish as a team.

Love Question:

What could a Love Our City week or day look like in your community? What projects could you do and who could you invite to serve with you?

Love Application:

How can you apply this to your life?

Love Notes:

What stuck out to you? What else is God saying to you?

Day 27

"Our Stories"

"In the same way, let your good deeds shine out for all to see, so that everyone will praise your heavenly Father."
- Matthew 5:16 NLT

"It was a total eclipse / of the heart / brand new start / no more clips of the dark / my life was canvas and the creator was making beautiful art / Like a beautiful mark / Here's the beautiful part / I found true peace at home / True peace alone / True peace is known / When you find that Jesus Christ is on the throne"
- Urban D. "Home" (Un.orthodox album)

There are so many God moments we've experienced from Love Our City week and Love Our City projects throughout the year. We use these projects and events to plant seeds. We are simply following the words of Jesus where we are taking care of the poor, the widows and the orphans. We are giving a cup of cold water in his name (we literally do with water bottle projects). Many times we may not be the ones that see those seeds grow. But, the more you keep loving your city, the more harvest you will begin to see unfold around you as the Holy Spirit begins to work in people's lives. We've seen lots of amazing stories and we believe there are many seeds that are still in the germinating process.

Jose came home from work and found his wife with a huge smile on her face as she shared about a church group that randomly brought a bag of groceries to their door that evening. She had been praying for a miracle as she was unsure how they would have enough food to make it through the week. God provided. The next day Jose went to work at his maintenance job at the mall. A group of people showed up from this same church and had appreciation gift bags for all forty-five employees. The bag included a candy bar, some gum, a handwritten note and a gift card for a sandwich. Nobody ever gave the maintenance men gift bags of appreciation. He was touched. Jose wanted to find out more about this church group and why they would do this. Even though Jose doesn't fluently speak English yet, he is now regularly attending Crossover Church.

Liz had recently been going through a rough season. She was at the gym when a young girl came up and invited her to the Love Our City celebration party coming up the next Sunday. Liz had been thinking about going back to church and this was a sign for her. When she showed up at Crossover Church that Sunday she immediately felt welcomed and God started doing something inside of her during the service. At the end she responded to the gospel and made a commitment to get right with God. We were having a spontaneous water baptism that day and I started sharing about making a public declaration of your faith through water baptism. She had never been baptized before and she was not planning on it, but as people started standing up and going down front she felt God's spirit pulling her, but she didn't move. I felt there were still a few more people that were going to respond, so we gave one more opportunity. Liz jumped out of her seat and ran down to the front as the church celebrated! She and 60 other people got baptized that Sunday. The next Sunday she started bringing her friend Luis who hadn't been to church in nearly two decades. They both went through the 3D Growth Track and officially became members. A few months later Liz joined our worship team and now you can regularly see her on the platform leading people into God's presence.

Our bus blessing project goes to the bus terminal to give out a free one-day bus pass along with a gift bag. It was actually the very first project of Crossover's Love Our City week 2018. So, we were all fired up and ready to reach people. There were so many people at the bus terminal that we were out of bus passes and gift bags in less than 15 minutes, but there were some God moments. I met Derek from Miami. He was a middle-aged guy that had just moved to Tampa a few months ago. Although he was happy to get a bus pass and gift bag he didn't seem very engaged at first. I asked a few questions about how he liked Tampa and what brought him here. He started to warm up and ask a few questions about what we were doing. I shared with him about the church and eventually I told him I was the lead pastor. There was suddenly a shift in the conversation at that point as he started asking me some deep spiritual questions about struggling to let go and let God take control. Here we were at the bus terminal and it was turning into this special ministry moment. I shared some of my spiritual journey and encouraged him. He grabbed my hand and said, "Thanks Pastor, I'll see you at church on Sunday." Sure enough, that Sunday after service he came up to me in the lobby and said, "Hey, you remember me?" Thank God I have a good memory (at least short term) and I said, "Hey! It's Derek from Miami – you came!" He was blown away that I remembered him and talked about how much he enjoyed the service and that he found his new church home.

Jalisa is a millennial that kept getting invited to church by her supervisor Jackson. She was hesitant as she hasn't been to church in a long time and the last time she went it was awkward. But, when he invited her to come serve on his team for Love Our City week this sparked her interest. She went with a group to the laundromat and paid for everyone's laundry. Jalisa loved seeing the surprise on people's faces and the conversations that followed. She got to meet several other church members and even one of the pastors at the event. They made her feel like family. Jalisa was so curious about the church she showed up at the celebration party and has regularly been attending ever since.

I had to add one more that I just heard a few days ago. My wife and I went to speak at our college Bible Study. Dozens of students were there and all but two or three of them are brand new to our church this year. God is doing something special with these students. We just baptized several of them a few weeks ago and one of those girls came up to me and started sharing what God was doing in her life. I asked her how she first started coming to our church. She was at the grocery store and someone with a Love Our City shirt gave her a gift card towards her groceries. They also invited her to Crossover. It took her a few weeks to finally come, but since then she has been there every week. I met her friend that has only been coming three weeks and she is now on fire for God and also got baptized. This exciting movement with our college students all traces back to Love Our City as even the guy now leading the ministry first came because he saw all of the people with T-shits serving in the neighborhood! I know you are going to have some amazing stories too! We'd love to hear them and share them! Contact us at www.loveourcitybook.com where we'll be sharing more stories. Let's celebrate what God is doing!

Love Lesson:

The more you keep loving your city, the more harvest you will begin to see unfold around you as the Holy Spirit begins to work in people's lives.

Love Question:
What is a great story of spiritual transformation that you have seen from showing the love of Christ to others?

Love Application:
How can you apply this to your life?

Love Notes:
What stuck out to you? What else is God saying to you?

Day 28

"Our Movement"

*"Feed the hungry, and help those in trouble.
Then your light will shine out from the darkness,
and the darkness around you will be as bright as noon."*
- Isaiah 58:10 NLT

*"When rebuilding there's seasons of growth and
forward movement / But there's times of plateau and
decline that's not in your blueprint"*
- Urban D. "Rebuilding Movement" (ReBuild album)

Although I may have written the book about Love Our City, I'm not the one who originated the idea of churches serving their communities. Churches have been doing similar things like this for centuries. Like King Solomon said, "There is nothing new under the sun." We take ideas and remix them for our context. Over the years we have seen several churches doing service projects and we were inspired and put our own spin on it. One of the churches that inspired us was a church plant that our church helped mentor. They did a residency internship with us. Our church's innovative ideas have helped many up and coming churches. As we help churches, they also help and inspire us. Their creativity and young zeal is contagious. They innovate and take big risks for God's kingdom. City life church in Lansing, Michigan is one of those churches that are crushing it.

City Life Church | *Jerome Vierling – Lead and Founding Pastor*

"We launched City Life Lansing, an Inner City Church Plant in Lansing MI. Talk is cheap and so many of our team knows what it is like to feel forgotten. Our heartbeat is to let the city know that Jesus loves the city! In the early months love the city was our anthem. In our first year we kicked off a "Love the city week". We put a goal in our first year to raise $20,000 to do as many acts of love in one week. The problem was we only had $4,000 and it was only three weeks away. Our people stepped up and Jesus knocked it out of the park. People are hungry to show the love of God in a real way.

We chose neighborhoods that fit our vision where we have long-term holistic ministry work. These are places where we were already tutoring, had people living near, and team members who are present there. It was a huge wide brush to paint with love. Pastor Brad Leach once said "Good works, leads to good will, which can lead to the Good News." We found that to be so true! We had an idea to clean a stranger's house. Well, it is a strange idea but we thought it would be neat and felt it was from Jesus... so here we go. One of our leaders (Rhett) was sent with the task to knock on doors and see if someone would let us clean. One amazing woman, Jenna said, "Maybe, I have to talk to my boyfriend first." The deadline was fast approaching for us to lock a house in and we needed a confirmation. Rhett followed up and she mentioned her boyfriend was quite skeptical and he then asked if I would go and maybe we could do some final persuasion. They ended up saying yes, especially when we told them, 'Hey we know this is kind of weird but we think Jesus wants us to do this for someone and he picked you.' That house cleaning changed their lives forever. They laughed and they came to City Life eventually. Not only did Jenna join our Dream Team but just this past month her boyfriend Jay got baptized and also joined the Dream Team as well.

We have a street in our town that many say is the worst in town. People say, "Don't go there or you will get shot." What people forget is where there are people, there are God's creation made in his image. So that is exactly where we went for our "Knock Knock" groceries night. We basically show up at someone's door and say, "Hey, we got some snacks and food for your Friday night, hope you enjoy!" We include a card that says, you are loved, belong and have purpose. We then invited them back to our weekend celebration. The night was ending and it was getting dark. One of our team members Lacey had one bag left and felt she needed go to one more house. This woman comes out and can't believe it. She goes on to say they are out of money, and that her assistance doesn't come for weeks and was just wondering what they would do. It was a sign for her that Jesus loved her and was listening. You can see it now, the tears, the hugs... but it didn't stop there. She came to church, got baptized, and is now greeting families on Sunday's at the main kids doors as a Dream Team member. What! Come on, Jesus! God was orchestrating divine timing over and over again. I hope this inspires you to keep loving your city, typing this reminds me too. Let's dream big, the Good News is better than we can imagine and a simple pack of gum and telling someone Jesus loves them can transformed their life forever."

There are churches that I regularly pour into and consult. As we started doing Love Our City week there were several others that learned from us and started one in their city. We're excited to see this movement grow to more and more cities.

The Edge Church | *Troy Evans – Lead and Founding Pastor*

"I serve as Pastor of a nine-year old urban church plant in Grand Rapids, MI called "The Edge". The past seven years Pastor Tommy has been a friend, coach and mentor for me. He has given me lots of advice and several strong "suggestions". I wish I could say that I implemented them as he instructed. I guess he caught me on a good day because when he challenged me to think about doing Love Our City, I could not stop thinking about this concept of no strings attached community engagement. Following our conversation we planned for five months and hosted our first "Love GR" event. During this event we were able to go show the love of Christ to business owners and residents in our surrounding community. We put a special emphasis on serving our local barbers and hair stylist, as we believe that in every urban community they are most forgotten for the life long services they provide. To see the expression on people's faces for a church to serve them coffee and donuts, give them a certificate of appreciation and pray for them was priceless. We hand delivered hundreds of plants to our residents. This year our community impact director had the idea to provide spa baskets to all the teachers in the school located next-door to our church. This year will be our 3rd year to implement it and we are looking forward to all that God will do through the seeds planted through this simple yet impactful outreach."

Love Lesson:

TThere is nothing new under the sun.
Take ideas and remix them for your own context.

Love Question:

Have you ever been part of a something great
that you watched spread and grow into a movement?

Love Application:

How can you apply this to your life?

Love Notes:

What stuck out to you? What else is God saying to you?

Citylife Church (Lansing, MI) & The Edge Church (Rapids, MI)

LOVE OUR CITY VIDEO SERIES: WEEK 4

Watch the video at www.youtube.com/urband813

As Believers in Christ we are called to _____ the atmosphere around us.

"Choose a good reputation over great riches; being held in high esteem is better than silver or gold." - Proverbs 22:1 NLT

We are called to be God's _Ambassadors_: A person who acts as a representative or a promoter.

Read 1 Corinthians 5:16-21

Is your APPEAL - _appealing_?

The way to get closer to God, step into your calling and truly love your city starts with _prayer_.

Betterment can do some good, but development is even better as it _teaches_ _empowers_ people to become self-sustainable and build their own capacity.

Getting someone out of poverty or brokenness is not an _____, it's a _____.

Discussion Questions

1. Have you ever seen the atmosphere shift when a solid Christian or several solid Christians came into the mix?
(At your job, or school, or in a family situation)

* *Read Proverbs 22:1*

2. What is the reputation of Christians & Churches in your community?

* *Read 1 Corinthians 5:16-21*

3. What could reconciliation look like in your city?

4. How does your appeal for God look? How can it improve?
(Get honest – it's the last session)

5. What does your regular prayer and devotional rhythm look like? How can it improve?

6. What are some ways you can give people a hand up in your city?

7. What is next for you, your group and your church now that Love Our City is finishing for this season?

Day 29

"Our Justice"

*"Learn to do good; seek justice, correct oppression;
bring justice to the fatherless, plead the widow's cause."*
- Isaiah 1:17 ESV

*"Check Nehemiah 5 he confronted injustice / Stood up for the
forgotten / We need to discuss this / Because our planet has a
leadership crisis / From Greece, to Russia, to China, to Isis"*
- Urban D. "Empowering Others" (ReBuild album)

That word "Justice" can cause some Christians to hesitate. There have been some social justice movements that emphasized good works and excluded the gospel. Justice is not meant to be a replacement of the gospel - it should be a result of the gospel. The definition of justice is "just behavior or treatment". If you have a relationship with Jesus, then we should have just behavior and treatment towards our neighbors. Why? Because justice is part of God's character. Psalm 33:5 (NIV) says, "The Lord loves righteousness and justice; the earth is full of his unfailing love." In Psalm 146:7 the scriptures tells us, "He gives justice to the oppressed and food to the hungry. The Lord frees the prisoners." The calling of Jesus was prophesied about in the Old Testament. He was called to bring justice. Matthew 12:18 quotes this prophecy about the Messiah as it says, "Look at my Servant, whom I have chosen. He is my Beloved, who pleases me. I will put my Spirit upon him, and he will proclaim justice to the nations."

We are called to bring justice to our neighbors. Let me remind you that it doesn't only mean the neighbors that look like us and think like us and are in the same economic bracket as us. It also means to the ones that are different than us. It even means the ones that are oppressed, hungry and in bondage. When Jesus shared the two greatest commandments He was quoting scripture from the Old Testament. The first verse is from Deuteronomy 6:5, and the second is from Leviticus 19:9-18. This passage in Leviticus goes into detail of how we should practice justice towards our neighbors around us in our city.

Imagine if we did these things:

* Live generously towards the poor and the foreigners. (vs.9-10)

* Don't steal. (vs. 11)

* Don't deceive or cheat anyone. (vs. 11)

* Don't defraud, rob or exploit people. (vs. 13)

* Don't disrespect deaf or blind people. (vs. 14)

* Don't twist justice by being partial to the poor or showing favor to the rich. Judge honestly. (vs. 15)

* Don't gossip. (vs. 16)

* Stand up for your neighbor when they are threatened. (vs. 16)

* Don't hate your brother or sister. (vs. 17)

* Don't seek revenge or hold a grudge, but love your neighbor as yourself. (vs. 18)

Did you know when we love our neighbors it actually fulfills the law? Paul mentions this twice in Romans 13:8-10 where it says, "Owe nothing to anyone – except for your obligation to love one another. If you love your neighbor, you will fulfill the requirements of God's law. For the commandments say, 'You must not commit adultery. You must not murder. You must not steal. You must not covet.' These – and other such commandments – are summed up in this one commandment: 'Love your neighbor as yourself.' Love does no wrong to others, so love fulfills the requirements of God's law." When Paul says owe nothing to anyone in context he is talking about our debts. It doesn't mean that we should never borrow anything. It doesn't mean we shouldn't borrow any money, but it means that we pay our taxes, our mortgages and our payments on time. We can pay those things down and pay them off. But our obligation to love one another is not something that we pay down or pay off. As Christians, it is something we are obligated to do. I know that word obligation can have somewhat of a negative vibe to it. But Paul is teaching us that every debt that can be paid off should be paid off with love. Turn every behavior into an act of love. Love for God turns into a visible manifestation when we love others. That is what biblical justice is all about!

Love Lesson:

Justice is not meant to be a replacement of the gospel - it should be a result of the gospel.

Love Question:

How can you better live out Isaiah 1:17 in your life?

Love Application:

How can you apply this to your life?

Love Notes:

What stuck out to you? What else is God saying to you?

Day 30

"Our Dream"

"I am in them and you are in me. May they experience
such perfect unity that the world will know that you sent me
and that you love them as much as you love me."
- **John 17:23 NLT**

"Imagine a city where churches work together / There's no
competition – just a kingdom endeavor / It gets no better / Imagine
impact you could measure / That goes beyond attendance at a
sermon or lecture"
- **Urban D. "New life, new fam, new city" (ReBuild album)**

Our dream should reflect Jesus' vision for the church when he prayed in John 17 that believers would be in complete unity so the world will know the love of God. To an outsider, Christ followers can seem divided at times. There are some Christ followers that are extremely conservative, some that are more liberal, some that are inward focused, some that are outward focused, some that are out of touch, some that are culturally relevant, some that are engaged in social justice, and some that are engaged in politics. We could go on and on listing the different styles, methods, passions, and theological leanings that Christians and churches have. All those differences are not always a bad thing, but dream with me for a minute... what if the capital C church was known for truly loving their cities? What if we were known for following the words of Jesus where we authentically loved our neighbors as ourselves? That is one thing we could rally around!

Unfortunately, in many communities the church can be viewed as a parasite. It comes in and sucks out resources. But what if the reputation of the church was different everywhere? What if it was positive? What if we were known for being a place that poured out resources? It could be known as a place to find healing, hope, friendships and answers. Imagine if Christians were known for bringing people together, empowering them, and making their communities a better place. Even people that don't agree with our message would still respect and appreciate the work that we do in our cities. The church should be a life source which radically makes its community better, both spiritually, and physically. Imagine if the city looked to the church for solutions when crisis and tragedy hit. I regularly challenge church leaders with the following questions: If your church closed its doors today would your neighborhood even notice? Would they care? Would it impact them?

We are seeing our dream slowly but surely come to fruition in our city in Tampa. As we continue to love our community the reputation of churches are growing more and more positive. Several pastors and Christian leaders are sitting in community leadership positions to help leverage change in policies and major redevelopment decisions happening our districts. The events and programs our churches put on are partnering with government and businesses to meet tangible needs like backpacks, school supplies, Christmas gifts, food, job training, job fairs, and more. The church is being invited to these positions because of the positive influence we have developed. It is also happening in several other cities around the world.

Our dream is that churches everywhere would get more involved in loving their city as they follow the instructions of Jesus. It goes way beyond a week of community service projects and a 30-day devotional book. Our dream is that this is a primer to get you set up to turn this into your new normal. We pray you will begin to look through new lenses at your everyday life and see opportunities all around you. Our dream is that this would become a multiplication movement that would go viral around the world. We believe this could be the beginning of the next great awakening of the church as we learn to Love Our City and point people to Jesus.

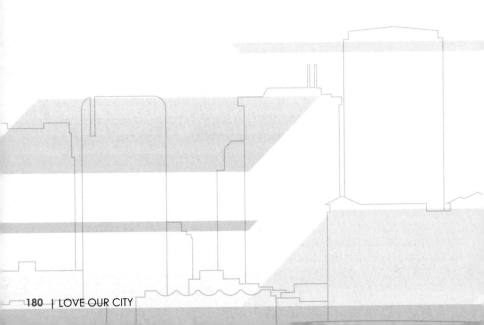

Love Lesson:

The church can be and should be a life source that radically makes the community better, both physically and spiritually.

Love Question:

If your church closed tomorrow would your community notice? How would it impact them?

Love Application:

How can you apply this to your life?

Love Notes:

What stuck out to you? What else is God saying to you?

Day 2:
[1] Linsay Wissman, "2017 Federal poverty level guidelines" www.peoplekeep.com - Feb. 7, 2017.

[2] Alison Doyle, "Average salary for U.S. workers" www.thebalancecareer.com - Aug. 14, 2018.

Day 4:
[1] "World's population increasingly urban with more than half living in urban areas" www.un.org - July 10, 2014.

[2] Bret Boyd, "Urbanization and the mass movement of people to cities." www.graylinegroup.com

[3] "UN: World population increasingly urban" www.cbsnews.com - Feb. 26, 2008.

[4] Claire Trapusso, "Reverse Migration: how baby boomers are transforming cities" www.realtor.com - May 17, 2016.

[5] Charlotte Alter, "Marjority of America's undocumented immigrants in 20 urban areas" www.time.com - Feb. 9, 2017.

[6] Valarie Strauss, "For the first time, minority students expected to be majority in U.S. public schools this fall" www.washingtonpost.com - Aug. 21, 2014.

[7] "The state of the American Church" www.malphursgroup.com

Day 8:
[1] German Lopez, "How the world went from 170 million to 7.3 Billion." www.vox.com - Jan. 30, 2016.

[2] www.populationinstitute.org

[3] "Census: Tampa Bay shows forth highest population growth in nation." www.tampabay.com - March 23, 2017.

[4] John Romano "Tampa Bay ranks low in religion census" www.tampabay.com - May 22, 2012.

Day 12:
[1] "WHO Library Cataloging-in-Publication Data: Global and regional estimates on violence against women" World Health Organization 2013.

[2] Caitlin Gibson, Emily Guskin, "A majority of Americans now say that sexual harassment is a 'serious problem'" www.washingtonpost.com - Oct. 17, 2017.

[3] Stephanie Zachrek, Eliana Dockterman, Haley Sweetland Edwards "Time Person of the Year – 2017" www.time.com

[4] www.rainn.org/statistics

[5] "The 1 in 6 statistic" – www.1in6.org

Day 13:
[1] Clark Mendock, "Americans throw away 150,000 tons of food everyday" www.independent.co.uk - April 4, 2018.

[2] "Consumption by the United States" www.public.wsu.edu

Day 18:
[1] Bill Easum, "10 church stats you need to know for 2018" www.reachrightstudios.com

[2] Mark Deymaz, "Outeach Magazine – Ethnic Blends" www.outreachmagazine.com/Deymaz

[3] Sam Eaton, "59% of millennials raised in church have dropped out – and they're trying to tell us why" www.faithit.com - April 4, 2018.

Day 19:
[1] Richard Alleyne, "Welcome to the information age – 174 newspapers a day" www.telegraph.co.uk - Feb. 11, 2011.

[2] ibid.

Day 23:
[1] Daniel Burke "Millennials leaving the church in droves, study finds" www.cnn.com - May 14, 2015.